Don't Die Broke

HOW ANNUITIES CAN GUARANTEE YOUR INCOME FOR LIFE AND KEEP YOUR RETIREMENT FROM GOING BELLY-UP

—

David J. Reindel

with STEVE MARSH

FOREWORD BY **Fran Tarkenton**

A B2 BOOK

CHICAGO

Printed in the United States.

Library of Congress Cataloging-in-Publication Data

Reindel, David J.
 Don't die broke : how annuities can guarantee income for life and keep your retirement from going belly-up / David J. Reindel, with Steve Marsh ; foreword by Fran Tarkenton.
     p. cm.
 Summary: "A guide to the use of annuities in retirement planning, focused on the needs of people whose retirement is rapidly approaching"--Provided by publisher.
 ISBN-13: 978-1-932841-49-7 (pbk.)
 ISBN-10: 1-932841-49-0 (pbk.)
 1. Annuities. 2. Retirement income--Planning. 3. Finance, Personal. I. Marsh, Steve, 1951- II. Title.

 HG8790.R45 2009
 368.3'7--dc22

                              2008054017

08 09 10 12 13   10 9 8 7 6 5 4 3 2 1

B2 Books is an imprint of Agate Publishing. Agate books are available in bulk at discount prices. For more information, go to agatepublishing.com.

TABLE OF CONTENTS

FOREWORD

WHEN DAVID REINDEL FIRST CAME TO ME WITH HIS manuscript, I didn't expect to fall out of my seat with excitement. Then I began to read *Don't Die Broke,* and I couldn't put it down until I'd read the very last word. What a vital message for consumers today, and for those in years to come.

I was honored when David asked me to write the foreword to *Don't Die Broke,* because it's a must-read for consumers, as well as every financial professional in this country. It has a loud and clear message about asset preservation that every American needs to hear—especially seniors. It offers more clear and concise reasons and methods for safe-retirement strategies than any other book I have ever read. Therefore, I know it will save retirement lifestyles by the tens of thousands—and maybe even yours.

Recall the often mindless euphoria of the late 1990s; the market crash of 2001; the subsequent downturns, corrections, recession; and the financial catastrophe that has resulted from the crisis of 2007–2008. Should we expect a continued rocky ride on Wall Street? Of course. Recessions and corrections are a predictable part of investment life, but the longer you live, the less likely you'll be to survive the realities of risk. Unfortunately, few of us ever prepare for a necessary change of investment strategy, which is what this book is all about.

David's book also serves as a great tonic to those potentially devastating "inside" tips on red-hot stocks and other tales of "unlimited upside potential." You've heard them all. The temptation can leave you in the poorhouse, and you know it. Yet I am constantly amazed

by the countless numbers of mature investors—especially people in
retirement—who cling to a 100 percent risk scenario. No wonder
so many were forced to go back to work after the 2001 crash and
the 2008 disaster in the financial sector, and we'll watch it happen
all over again in the coming years. It will be as if the crisis markets
of 2001 and 2008, and countless points between, never happened
at all.

That's why I'm happy to step forward and endorse the message in
this book. For decades we've lived in a trance of Wall Street tradition,
mesmerized by the rule of "taking necessary risks to reap rewards."
Countless numbers of investors have tossed and turned, night after
night, because we've been conditioned to live in fear by traders who
reap fortunes in commissions on our trades. So some of us "stay the
course" with risk until it's too late—and that's too bad.

Don't Die Broke presents the real truth: There are safe-retirement
alternatives that aren't bedeviled by fear and greed. It's that simple. As
average and even sophisticated investors alike suffer enormous financial losses in the market, a barrage of disinformation continues. But
it's nothing more than pro-risk hype fed by moguls in the securities
industry, stock-pumping radio and TV personalities, and other so-
called "experts" who fill people with adrenaline-based market fever
well into their sixties—until catastrophic losses hit them squarely in
the portfolio.

For those who are over fifty-five, and even younger people who
are interested in a safe-retirement scenario, David Reindel highlights
asset preservation and income guarantees. In *Don't Die Broke,* he finally says what many of us have been trying to say since the late
1990s, when an overvalued market spelled big trouble on the horizon: risk is a very poor security blanket for retirement. After a certain
age, it's all about protecting assets and ensuring guaranteed income,
and David shows you how to get there, right now.

In this book, you will examine risk and put it in a new light.
So if you enjoy playing a little Wall Street roulette, *caveat emptor.*
David just adds a few new tools to your financial plan. I like to call
them "secret weapons" that guarantee a safe, comfortable retirement
lifestyle—no matter what—and they include annuities and other in-

struments that have been around a long time. But now, they come with increased flexibility, better earnings, and more innovation than ever before, all of which you will discover in the pages of *Don't Die Broke.*

—*Fran Tarkenton*

INTRODUCTION

Who I Am ... and How I Can Help You Avoid the Poorhouse in Retirement

L ET'S BEGIN WITH WHO I AM IN RELATION TO WHERE *YOU* MAY BE in the next phase of your personal financial plan. By now, you've probably heard about the many players in the realm of financial planning. You might have been referred to stock and commodities brokers, reverse-mortgage specialists, estate-planning attorneys, life-insurance agents, certified financial planners, and an array of other broad-based "specialists" purporting to help in virtually every phase of retirement planning.

To set the record straight, I would never claim to be a one-stop source for all things financial. Like other annuity professionals, I have a team of specialists at hand should a need arise in areas beyond my expertise. But you should know that I specialize in one thing: a commodity known as the annuity—primarily the **fixed annuity**— and I know my business well.

I have another, less quantifiable quality, as well. Any longtime client of mine would likely tell you about my absolute concern for clients' individual financial futures. This passion eventually led me to specialize in the safety and security of the high-quality fixed annuity.

Why? Because fixed annuities are more than just investments. Unlike stocks, bonds, real property, and other instruments, the annuity preserves assets against loss in volatile financial markets and economies. Yet the annuity is also more than just a basic bank account earning minimal interest. A quality fixed annuity provides substantial future **income** while protecting and preserving your original principal.

That is, in a nutshell, the power and the strategic simplicity of the fixed annuity, and I have come to cherish that power. In volatile economic environments, I have seen the fixed annuity preserve critical retirement assets. While stocks and bonds have lost millions in market value in recent years, I've watched fixed annuities preserve lifestyles for my clients until the market could regain stability.

Today, I enjoy the satisfaction of incorporating appropriate fixed annuities into diversified asset portfolios. Such portfolios may contain a variety of investment assets, estate-planning instruments and other retirement vehicles, all provided by highly qualified specialists in many professional fields. But the fixed annuity can establish the real bedrock of your portfolio—the safe-haven preservation of your annuity-based **principal**.

I don't claim to be an expert in every field, and no truly seasoned professional should make such claims either. The best of us know how to work together to help you achieve your yearly financial goals and eventual retirement dreams. I enjoy those professional relationships, knowing my contribution may be one of the most essential cornerstones of a good retirement plan.

True annuity specialists are unique in the financial planning world because of the durability of our expertise. Here's what that means: Take my advice and shop it around. You will quickly find that I know the business of annuities well, and nothing puts clients more at ease than the confidence that their advisor has a thorough knowledge of virtually every type of annuity product available. In the hands of a truly qualified annuity professional, complex questions receive easy-to-understand answers. Individualized solutions are based on years of real, hands-on experience helping people handle their retirement scenarios.

Some of my clients liken me to a caregiver, but I consider myself more of a builder. Good financial planners build strong personal relationships in the process of really getting to know people, including their lifestyle goals and their related financial needs in the not-so-distant future.

That said, I'll segue to the rest of this book's content. Because it is a financial jungle out there, I will tell you about the trip wires, traps, and pitfalls in not only the annuity field but in the greater financial arena as well.

Of course, I will tell you why I favor quality fixed annuities, and what separates them from the rest. I will also tell you about the necessity of diversification and quality guidance in other fields. And I will give you the real truth, including cautions, about placing your money in any kind of savings account, asset preservation vehicle, or investment.

In addition to my identity as a relationship builder, I consider myself a professional income planner. The absolute worst thing you can do is to bury your cash savings in a mattress, so you must instead make prudent moves to grow and preserve your assets while ensuring the pace of its growth against inflation and market erosion. My job is to match client needs with income sources and protect them against market shortfalls as they come and go.

Many other financial professionals make the same or similar claims. Unfortunately, too many people in the field simply follow their own methodologies without really listening to their clients. Such practices run rampant in my industry.

Successful financial professionals become successful because they know how to listen. Their clients know it, and they tend to pass it on. In order to be a good listener, you have to ask the right questions and be qualified and ready to understand the answers. This is no easy task. It takes some financial professionals years to design questions that get at the heart of clients' needs and wishes. People at my professional level have honed that skill. We carefully listen to the answers our clients give us, because we know it's the only way we can begin to recognize their income needs.

How I Differ from Other Planners

As serious as I may seem, I have been a maverick throughout my career. When I began my career in life insurance in the 1970s, I received company-sponsored training in cash-value life insurance sales. Company-sponsored training (also called in-house training) was standard at the time, long before companies started outsourcing their training services. Today, various different contract training facilities offer a wide variety of training methodologies.

In the beginning, however, I accepted the in-house company training at face value. I was wide-eyed and eager to succeed, as many people are in the beginning. In fact, not I, nor any of the fellow trainees around me, ever bothered to question the substance of our training or the quality of the products we were trained to represent.

After the training, however, I began to contemplate these questions. I was determined to build my business in a logical, methodical manner based on product study and comparison—including the study of products other than those offered by the company that trained me. I also had questions about some of the company's sales training methods, but even more important were my questions about the fine-print details and features of the products I'd been trained to sell. I quickly realized that I hadn't been given straight and complete answers for some of the questions I had posed to my instructors.

I have to admit that I initially deceived myself about the training I'd received. From the word go, the training sessions left me with more questions than answers. Whenever I'd been given a problem to solve in college, I knew I could always ask my professors for the problem's solution to compare with my own answer. This prepared me to question any absence of solid answers in the real world. In the same sense, you should ask questions and expect your advisors to give you solid answers that make sense to you.

At that point, I felt compelled to strike out on my own and find those answers to generally enhance my own education. I'd been an avid reader and researcher in my college years, and the same quest for knowledge followed me into the insurance business. I read everything I could get my hands on about the industry, from trade journals to competing product manuals to additional textbook materials. Perhaps you've heard the adage that too much knowledge can get you into trouble. I think that was definitely true for me. My reading led me to reports with unsettling news; in particular, I discovered that some of the cash-value insurance products we'd been trained to sell were questionable, as were the sales techniques we'd been urged to accept as an industry norm.

From a variety of sources, I also confirmed that the company's cash-value life insurance policies were too expensive to be cost effective. In addition, the policies failed to provide adequate insurance coverage, and the sales commissions were quite high for a reason. Companies offering less than cost-effective policies and shoddy coverage were essentially bribing greedy salespeople to sell their products, which virtually always benefit the company and not the consumer. (Unfortunately, similar products are still around today.)

I didn't have to be an astute mathematician to put two and two together. The more I researched the criticism, the more I was convinced that the critics were right. The critics accurately demonstrated that greater life insurance coverage and better returns could be had through a combination of **term life insurance** and annuities: a term life policy costs much less, and the difference saved could be invested in other financial instruments, such as annuities, for higher returns.

The company wanted us to represent cash-value life insurance products as being both insurance policies and "investments," which is a claim no longer represented by ethical companies and salespeople. Why? Because insurance policies are not investments. Clients pay premiums through the years and, in return, their insurance policies can give them income in time of need. By contrast, investments can make or lose money. That's the difference.

Suggesting that an insurance policy is an investment suggests that policies share moneymaking features similar to those of stocks or bonds. That's simply not true. Therefore, the term "investment" is no longer used when referring to insurance policies. This may sound like hair-splitting to some people, but it's an ethical issue to people like me and others who share my vision of an ethical practice. Any kind of terminology that may even inadvertently mislead someone should be stricken from the vocabulary of an ethical insurance professional. As an industry advocate, I've worked hard to promote that kind of thinking, which has finally begun to take hold in our industry.

Critics back then often claimed that cash-value insurance salespeople lacked adequate training. They even said we were generally dishonest, which hurt me deeply. I have always driven myself to maintain the utmost credibility through honest business practices, and I have always adhered to the same honesty in my personal relationships. I don't play games with people, because for me, honesty is the essence of caring, and it's also the essence of real success in business. It's as simple as that.

Even today, I think it's wrong to say that the students who took this training with me were dishonest. Most were simply naive, accepting the artfully crafted sales methodology of trainers and seasoned company officials who might have been less than ethical. The students themselves were deceived into thinking their trainers were passing along traditional selling techniques, so they figured there was no need to question company products and tactics.

Many insurance people back then were too caught up in greed. Most insurance agents would not sell term policies or annuities because the commissions were comparatively low. So imagine the reaction I received from the company's sales managers when I insisted on selling only consumer-friendly annuities and term insurance policies. I became something of a thorn in the company's side. But I maintained that acting in the client's best interest—at the cost of a few dollars for myself—would eventually be balanced out by attracting more business through referrals from happy customers.

My sales managers didn't want to hear any such thing. They wanted their salespeople to hawk products earning maximum profits. They didn't care much about the long-term careers of individual sales reps or their reputations down the road. For that very reason, many good people wash out of the insurance business today. After all, how can one sustain a lifelong career by making inappropriate and unethical recommendations to customers? Eventually, word gets around.

My mathematician's logic told me I had no choice. If I wanted to succeed in the long term, I had to do the very best for my clients at all times or quit the business altogether. The alternative was a loss for the client and a career roadblock for me as a salesperson. But the decision cost me: even though I was moving more product, commissions from term insurance and annuities were far lower, which caused my income to drop considerably.

I struggled for a time, and company managers developed an increasingly unfavorable attitude toward me and my stubborn determination to do the right thing. Some even chuckled when my less-than-enviable paychecks were delivered, but times and trends began to turn away from the cash-value policy. People awoke to the realities I'd seen from the beginning, and some insurance companies gradually began to respond by developing new products. **Universal life insurance**, for example, offered more insurance coverage, better cash-value buildup, and a great deal of additional flexibility with respect to contract provisions. It was considered quite an innovation and may be appropriate for some people today.

For the record, I had nothing to do with those early consumer-friendly innovations, but I was proud of myself for recognizing the truth and holding fast to the only obvious course the industry would eventually have to take. The future lay in more consumer-friendly insurance products, and that early revelation helped shape my career.

I've remained something of a maverick to this day. These days, much of the industry remains sales and company oriented, but people at my end of the spectrum maintain a relationship-oriented business—we feel compelled to act in the client's best interest. While it irks me that some people have become successful working against the customer, I get a lot of satisfaction knowing that my voice has found some influence in the insurance industry as a whole. Industry leaders are listening to me, finally, and ideas, attitudes, and policies are changing for the better. After years of customer advocacy in this business, I can finally influence the way products are developed. I've also gained some clout when it comes to the way people are trained to sell those products and how salespeople train their customers to use them.

Why am I heard? Where did my industry influence come from? Answer: From acting in my clients' best interest. Amazing? Incredible? Nope. It's just common sense. Yet problems remain in the annuity business, and I am happy to discuss those problems with anyone willing to listen, from media people to top insurance-industry executives. I'm particularly driven to reach the executives who have the power to implement much needed reform. Insurance companies that offer the best products and services have discovered profit and affirmed that client-favorable honesty can be good business, period. Oddly enough, others still don't get it.

Regardless, my experience and success make me a formidable source of debate for industry opponents, and I applaud the opportunity to respond to annuity critics. I tend to agree with much of what the latter have to say, but so many necessary facts and truths get lost in the shuffle of media coverage. I often find myself backtracking to reeducate the misinformed before launching forward to discuss the real behind-the-scenes challenges facing our industry. I will examine some of those issues in Chapter 5.

CHAPTER 1

The Annuity Industry
and Safe-Retirement Advocacy

A S SOME OF MY PROFESSIONAL COLLEAGUES TUNED OUT A RISING chorus of criticism about the insurance business, I chose instead to listen closely to the critics. That listening process helped me understand the basis of their criticism, and as a result I, and others like me, have been able to hone our skills in the field of financial planning. Not every planner chose that goal. Some led their clients to high risk and soaring returns, but too many of the same went down in flames, leaving the business altogether and their clients' portfolios in smoking ruins.

Ironically, we financial planners have been equally critical of the insurance industry. We have challenged the industry to develop products that better serve the needs of clients rather than the needs of the industry itself, and this road hasn't always been smooth. But the rewards have come back to us through referrals from grateful clients and a resulting increase in business quantity and client quality. Amazingly enough, it has taken some coaxing to pass it on and convince insurance providers that today's client is more savvy than ever before—and that a more client-favorable product leads to more sales and increased (as opposed to decreased) revenues for the provider!

This concept comes full circle at a time when millions of baby boomers are at or near retirement. If some are fortunate enough to foresee the possibility of immediate retirement—due to the consistent performance of stock and bond funds in their individual retirement accounts (IRAs) and 401(k)s—those lucky few know what it took to get them to that enviable point.

Others haven't been so lucky. Many in the market developed a yen for risk during their younger earning years. They heard the mantra of risk from financial celebrities in the mass media without hearing the downside risk disclaimers. They came to believe that in order to get rich, or at least to attain enough wealth to retire, they would have to pack their portfolios with stocks and bonds.

This may sound like a broad generalization, so let's review the stats of recent trends: In the mid-1980s, it was widely acknowledged that only one in five, or 20 percent, of American households invested in the stock market. By mid-2007, roughly half of all American households had some kind of investment in the stock market.

I believe that this 30 percent gain in two decades from the so-called "consumer" sector of the economy arose from the onslaught of financial media and, to some degree, its charismatic celebrity superstars. That, and an ever-increasing awareness of the occasionally sensationalized risk-based opportunities available on Wall Street, helped drive the consumer sector of the market. But did every consumer understand the end game: the edge-of-retirement consequence of risk? After all, these consumers had traditionally busied themselves with purchases of automobiles, groceries, and appliances and had left the management of their retirement planning portfolios to some distant corporate entity.

Suddenly, thanks to a new generation of media-driven excitement about securities and some standout tales of success, everyone seemed to be jumping into the securities market. At the same time, many formerly average consumers got excited enough to take crash-course training programs and become overnight financial planners themselves.

From the latter, a new generation of investors accepted all sorts of iffy advice—grabbing additional nuggets from TV tipsters and a growing field of money blogs and popular financial publications. This was fine when we had plenty of earning years ahead of us. We had fewer assets to risk and less in general to lose, so we poured as much as we could afford—basically betting the farm of our discretionary income—into all sorts of mutual funds, IRAs, 401(k)s, and individual stocks and bonds.

Then came the traumatic market debacle of 2000–2001, when the aforementioned questionable advice turned into catastrophic losses for many. Portfolio values tumbled. Yet some consumer-level investors came away with enough assets to hang on to the possibility of retirement today.

You've probably heard the old adage that the Wall Street market is driven by two primordial emotions—fear and greed. Anyone cultivating a retirement portfolio in those heady years knew those emotions all too well. With our favorite media financial gurus cheering us onward, we learned to accept certain necessary risks. Yet it seemed as if our national consumer behavior had been modified to accept such risk, encouraged by the Pavlovian gratification—or even little more than the rumor of such gratification—of that occasional stratospheric gain.

Remember the fast-track 35 percent annual return on a meteoric tech stock? Remember the name of that stock, its paltry profit-to-earnings ratio, its post–research and development product that was going to set the world on fire—and never actually came to be? How about the computer-programmers-turned-overnight-day-traders in the fearless flush of the late-nineties market boom? Well, many barely recovered from the post–9/11 punishment only to find much more punishment to come. We let greed overtake fear in seemingly unstoppable markets and then we felt the pain of cyclical reality. We learned what our grandparents learned from the sudden brutality of the stunning market crash of 1929. After the greatest market crash in recent history—certainly the most disastrous crash in our lifetimes—many of our retirement dreams collapsed with the market.

Now, as we approach or enter our retirement years, we no longer have many working years ahead of us. While some securities advocates still insist that we need to stay in a 100 percent risk environment—to "stay the course," lest we outlive our retirement funds—I believe most of us share a bit of anxiety as we consider that advice. After all, we listened to disturbingly similar bromides before the crash of 2007–2008, and I am here to tell you that safe, solid alternatives to risk exist. There truly are methods to eradicate financial "sleepless nights" forever. I know you know what I'm talking about, because we've been around long enough to watch it happen, time and again.

Yet today, I also believe that we are no longer the same people who followed the stock market frenzy before the crash. Now we know—first hand—the desperation of seeing retirement plans turn to dust with market declines. We also know we have precious few years to recover from the punishment of this gigantic so-called "correction" that has been followed by one gut-wrenching roller coaster ride after another.

I think we've seen a dramatic paradigm shift in personal values, especially among the crowd of consumer investors. I think many of us now put fear ahead of greed, so I decided to write down the essentials of a professional belief system you won't often see talked up on TV. The following pages indeed reflect the sentiments of that growing professional voice, a contingent made up of some of the best people in this business, people who truly strive to help you preserve your assets through safe, secure, and risk-averse financial planning.

We haven't yet enjoyed the glitzy press coverage, maybe because conservative asset preservation strategies aren't sexy enough for prime time. But people are beginning to listen, and I am proud to say that I have been lucky enough to emerge as a leading voice in our growing movement, our "Quiet Revolution."

In this revolution, you won't hear anyone screaming about hot stocks or insider tips in the tech sector. You will, however, hear a unified voice of reason, which will help retrain your thinking to overcome the costly emotions of greed and fear. Once that's conquered, and you know that you will always have a safe, secure cache of retirement income, you might even discover recession-resistant new methods of growing your discretionary gains.

Either way, in the following pages I will help you discover our Quiet Revolution—we call it "safe-retirement planning"—and a quality lifestyle secured by guaranteed income you simply cannot outlive. For many, that simple goal has become a proven treasure.

CHAPTER 2

This Is Where YOU Come in:
Trading Securities Risk for Guaranteed Security

A S I'VE TOLD MANY CLIENTS, IT IS INDEED A JUNGLE OUT THERE. My voice was lost in a jungle of conjecture for a time. So were the admonitions of others like me. We warned of over-inflated values and market indices rocketing skyward on projections of endless prosperity. The good news is that we've learned a collective lesson, and the market is now filled with wiser consumers.

When we plan our retirement incomes, we now appreciate the fact that pension income can be guaranteed for life, and we take less comfort in the so-called guarantees of future Social Security payments. We also may listen less intently to every media tip, becoming a bit more skeptical of those who insist we entrust a lion's share of our assets to the volatility of stock and bond markets.

As we age, we learn something about overconfidence in over-stated assets and profit potential found in certain annual reports of yore. In short, much of today's investor confidence may be tempered by past experience. Even young investors who are new to the market have the benefit of experiencing the perilous fall first hand. In other words, when the market goes down, word goes 'round.

So how do we stay in the game and mitigate the pain? This is where you come in. Some call those of us in the Quiet Revolution the "Middle Men and Women" because we represent the middle ground between fear and greed. We feel that emotional middle ground is the place we'll find peace of mind and a secure retirement. Freedom from fear and greed can be found in a financial middle ground between two extremes. Any athlete—any top performer at all—will tell you this is true. If you reach too hard or too fast for the brass ring, it will surely slip away. Recoil in fear from the same brass ring and you will never find it. When we are controlled by emotional extremes in the financial realm, we lose control of ourselves and our immediate and long-term environments. We lose the essential shape and substance of our retirement dreams.

Let me put it another way: If we succumb to fear, we might avoid taking even the most moderate risk and sacrifice any opportunity for higher returns. The typical victim of this scenario thinks she hides in the haven of a standard savings account, but in truth, taxes may overtake any gains from the account, and they may eventually move in to erode his principal. If taxes don't, inflation certainly will, and the same thing happens if you stuff your cash savings in a mattress.

As for greed, we may find ourselves chasing risky investments. Recalling the "bubble" years of the late '90s, some of us keep hoping for a lifesaving windfall. Otherwise thoughtful and intelligent people are thus strapped to unrealistic expectations, visualizing a sustainable rate of return through their retirement years. While I wish them the best of luck—and it will take sheer luck—I've seen so many become consumed both by greed and an irrational fear of failure (a perceived failure to grab the perfect hot stock tip, that is). Virtually consumed by the paradoxical emotions of fear and greed, they live in apprehensive misery most of the time.

Middle Men and Women of the Quiet Revolution can enter this type of client's financial picture and keep warring emotions in check. Then, fear and greed leave the playing field and allow the client to work with a qualified advisor to plan a satisfying retirement.

What Is an Annuity?

The older you get, the less risk you should have. It may be appropriate for a thirty-year-old to invest in growth company stocks, which could appreciate rapidly. But if they go belly-up, the thirty-year-old has a long time horizon to earn his money back. Obviously, if a seventy-year-old did the same thing, he would face an enormous amount of risk. You know where I'm going with this: as you grow older, annuities become more and more important to your retirement plan. We will explore the annuity in greater detail throughout this book, but as a general overview, the annuity essentially works as an insurance policy for your money, and it also allows your money to grow and provide lifetime income. But what kind of annuity is more appropriate for you? How do annuities differ? How do they work?

It all begins when you make an initial contribution to the annuity, which we in the industry call **principal**—the principal contribution to the annuity account. (You're probably quite familiar with insurance **premiums**, such as those that are paid monthly by policyholders to maintain health insurance coverage.) Once you initiate a fixed annuity with a lump-sum contribution of principal, that principal is safely preserved. Guaranteed preservation of principal is indeed one of the vital functions of the fixed annuity—meaning that your principal will never be lost or at risk while safely inside the annuity account.

As for the annuity contract, like any other contract, this one comes with legal terminology defining **surrender charges**, the **rate of interest earnings** to be accumulated under the provisions of the annuity contract, various features, contract **riders**, and other elements that make annuities flexible and capable of providing income for life.

But first, let's talk a bit about income, which is what the annuity holder typically receives after the annuity matures (although the annuity marketplace does offer several flexible variations of income **payout schedules**). Income may be received in several different ways depending on the contract holder's preference, including a steady monthly payout for the rest of the his life. Depending on how the annuity is structured, this income may indeed actually exceed the amount of principal and accumulated earnings of the original annuity. Thus, the annuity owner's total monthly income payment can be based on the owner's age and other factors at the time she begins receiving her first income payouts.

We'll explore this in more detail later in the book, but such income begins with the accumulation of interest credits, or interest **earnings**, which are monies continually added to the annuity owner's account as interest based on the annuity owner's principal contribution accumulates.

From time to time, you will also hear the term **accumulation value**. This is simply the total amount of money accumulated to date from the accumulating monies added to the annuity owner's account. While accumulation value initially grows from interest gained from the annuity owner's original contribution to the annuity, it continues to grow beyond that point from the added compounded earning power of continuously accumulated earnings added to principal. Later in this book, I provide tables that show how annuities grow your total accumulation value from principal.

Let's take a moment to talk about the different kinds of annuities available in this evolving marketplace.

The traditional annuity. **Traditional annuities** were commonplace in the portfolios of our parents and grandparents. Purchased for a defined period of time, these annuities divulged the annuity's rate of interest for the first year—and the first year only! All subsequent annual rates of interest were unknown for the remainder of the contract period. If, for example, you purchased a seven-year annuity (a traditional norm), the insurance carrier might give you a 6 percent guarantee, but only for the first year of the annuity's overall performance. At the beginning of the second year, you would receive a written notice from the insurance carrier informing you about the rate of return for the coming year.

In short, people were essentially left in the dark by the carrier and were often given only a bare minimum of guaranteed return. That was during another, more trusting, era. Annuities have since progressed and modernized to provide far more earnings, guarantees, and (unfortunately) complexities, which can be abused by unscrupulous salespeople.

The traditional annuity is built to preserve principal over a period of time and may not be appropriate for everyone. It is appropriately structured to include various charges that are fair and equitable to the consumer, especially in consideration of the measures providers must take to insure annuity buyers' principal and income—particularly during economic hard times.

Immediate annuities. **Immediate annuities** are also called **single-premium income annuities (SPIAs)**. SPIAs can provide a lifetime of income for an annuity policyholder, income for a specific amount of time, or a number of other variations. Payouts for any or all combinations begin from a month to a year after the policyholder contributes a one-time deposit. Payout schedules can be set up for monthly, quarterly, semiannual, or annual payments.

Multiyear guaranteed annuities. The **multiyear guaranteed annuity (MYGA)** resembles a bank certificate of deposit (CD) in that it offers a specific, guaranteed rate of return for a designated time period, perhaps 6 percent a year for five years. After five years, the annuity's owner may cash out and walk away or renew at a new rate. This type of instrument is ideal for someone who wants to maintain a degree of liquidity at a guaranteed rate, which often exceeds standard interest rates offered through bank CDs. However, be sure to compare surrender charges attached to the MYGA as opposed to early withdrawal fees for a bank CD. The surrender charge could be considerably higher, because such charges may be attached to an MYGA annuity with higher earnings.

The fixed annuity. The **fixed annuity** offers a guaranteed rate of earnings each year. These earnings are added to the initial, or principal, contribution to the annuity. The fixed annuity guarantees that the principal contribution cannot be lost, and the rate of annual earnings being added to the fixed annuity is also guaranteed. Unlike the fixed-indexed annuity, earnings in a fixed annuity contract may not be directly affected by market index activity.

The fixed-indexed annuity. The **fixed-indexed annuity** accumulates earnings over a set time period. However, unlike other annuities that offer a set rate of future interest credits, the fixed-indexed annuity determines the annuity owner's annual interest credits according to the performance of various stock market indices in a given year, and every year during the multiyear period (also known as the **accumulation cycle**), the fixed-indexed annuity will accumulate earnings for the annuity account.

At the same time, the fixed-indexed annuity may also offer a fixed minimum rate of interest earnings each year—perhaps 1 percent. The insurance carrier meanwhile reinvests client premiums, which are backed by government-mandated reserves, and the results of those investments determine the level of interest credits the annuity owner would receive above the "fixed minimum rate of interest earnings" in a given year. The carrier will also impose a cap on owner earnings, which certainly limits the upside earning potential for the annuity owner when the market is healthy and rising. In exchange, the owner reduced her risk of market exposure.

Let's say the annuity owner chooses to go with an **earnings cap** of 9.5 percent and the full market increase turns out to be 12 percent for the year. In this scenario, the annuity owner's gain would be 9.5 percent, which would be added to the principal and locked in. Every indexed increase is locked in and compounded on an annual basis. If the market is negative, there is no increase, but there is also no loss to the current balance. On the customer side of the ledger, some annuity contracts provide that such gains are credited as annual **resets** of the customer's annuity account, with some contracts calling for resets every two, four, or even five years, but resets of five years are less common.

The insurance companies put a large portion of any premiums in bonds, like any other annuity. Next, they take a small portion of the premiums and purchase options in various indexes. The charge for the options will vary from year to year, depending on various economic considerations, such as interest rates and market volatility.

The primary debate revolving around the fixed-indexed annuity is whether or not it should be considered a security and thus be regulated by the U.S. Securities & Exchange Commission (SEC). Some believe this type of annuity should remain under the purview of the insurance industry and treated as an insurance product, thus ensuring that it would continue to be fairly represented by insurance advocates. I'm firmly planted in the middle of the debate, advocating that it should remain available to insurance sellers. After all, why would a risk-based stock market advocate sell a risk-mitigating product like a fixed-indexed annuity, especially if the ongoing cycle of securities trading gains the market advocate far more in total commissions?

However, unlike many others in the insurance industry, I also want people who sell fixed-indexed annuities to have some kind of stock-market orientation and related regulation under the aegis of the SEC. This would be the case if everyone who represented fixed-indexed annuities were additionally licensed as **registered investment advisors (RIAs)**.

In the past, you may have heard of an **equity-indexed annuity**. Today's fixed-indexed annuity and the equity-indexed annuity are essentially the same thing. However, the word "equity" is a misnomer, because it implies that the annuity may be some kind of equity product; it is not. Fixed-indexed annuities are insurance products that offer consumers the option to choose how they would like to have their annuity-account earnings credited on an annual basis. They may elect to have their annuity credited according to the performance of a chosen index, or they may allocate all or part of their earnings at a fixed interest rate for the year. They are also able to reallocate their funds on an annual basis as they wish every year on their contract's anniversary.

Variable annuities. As a general rule, fixed-indexed annuities are quite safe, but you should carefully inspect them for various fees and features. Each fixed-indexed annuity product differs. **Variable annuities** are not particularly safe, in my opinion. Most recent criticism aimed at annuities has been aimed at the variable annuity; fees tend to be higher for variable annuities, for example, and guarantees that are included at no charge with a fixed annuity can be costly with a variable. And of course, some of us question whether a variable annuity is simply a package of securities wrapped in an annuity contract. My primary complaints against variable annuities are the layers of fees and risk—returns vary with the variable annuity, so why not go for risk and higher returns with stocks and mutual funds?

While I don't generally use variable annuities in my own practice, we hear enough about them to warrant some explanation of how they work. As media people sometimes suggest, they carry a degree of risk that I believe might be more effectively managed through other investments. Variables might have a place in the portfolio of a younger consumer who has a significant amount of working years ahead of her. But to eventually see a lifetime income stream or future lump-sum payment, those working years may be necessary to recover any securities market losses related to the investment activities of variable annuity carriers.

A variable annuity might initially be purchased with the payment of a lump sum of cash, which is otherwise known as the payment of a **single premium**. The variable annuity might also be funded continuously with periodic infusions of cash deposits, which are then applied to the annuity contract. Either way, your cash goes into something called an **accumulation unit**, which is actually a small piece of the insurance company's overall investment portfolio. Here's how it works: Say an insurance company's portfolio is worth $20 million. If the company decides to split up its $20 million into four million separate accumulation units, each unit would be worth $5. As investment advisors hired by the insurance company increase the worth of the company's portfolio, each accumulation unit accordingly increases in value. For example, if the portfolio grows from $20 million to $25 million, the accumulation units would grow from being worth $5 to being worth $6.25 each.

Not at all unlike the asset allocation packages offered through mutual funds, variable annuities may offer only one or several different combinations of financial vehicles for consumers to choose from. The asset mix could include anything from money-market funds to bonds or other types of securities. But that brings up yet another need for consumer caution with variable annuities: the mixed bag of vehicles in the variable may, and often do, vary widely in terms of risk, overall quality of performance, profit/loss ratios, and other factors common among instruments in the securities market. Thus, you should consult someone who is licensed to sell securities and is also highly skilled in this area to help you select appropriate investments for your variable annuity.

You ultimately choose the mix of investments in a variable annuity based on your own level of risk tolerance, and you buy accumulation units accordingly. In this arena, investors have a lot of choices, and the performance of the variable annuity has come under fire in recent years as a result. A well-managed, growth-oriented stock portfolio might offer a much better alternative for more risk-tolerant investors. More conservative investors could also choose a portfolio of high-quality bonds to avoid the volatility of short-term investment, and keep a portion of funds in a money-market account as well. The choices of risk are many, and they all involve a degree of exposure my customers tend to avoid. That's why I cannot and do not recommend investment in a variable annuity.

Variable annuity accounts rise and fall along with securities-market activity, making them unsuitable for the portfolios of many seniors. In addition, variable annuities come with a variety of fees, which may significantly reduce the value of the overall variable annuity account. And that reduction equates to a reduction of your ultimate investment return. Therefore, seniors in particular need to be fully aware of not only the risk associated with a variable annuity, but also the following fees and charges.

Surrender charges are a reality with most variable annuities. As with fixed annuities, surrender charges for early withdrawal can be costly within certain time periods following an initial contribution. Those periods tend to range from three to ten years or more, so you're not just committing to the downside risk of the variable annuity— you also assume the risk of significant early withdrawal penalties if market downturns spell trouble for the variable annuity's performance. That means you'll lose in a down market, and you'll lose if you try to get out. Meanwhile, some of the surrender charge goes toward the payment of a commission to the financial representative who sold you the variable annuity in the first place.

All of the above can be particularly aggravating to the investor, even though some variable annuity contracts allow the usual 10 to 15 percent annual penalty-free withdrawal of the value of the account. Unlike fixed annuities, which retain all former gains and original principal, the variable annuity is subject to an agonizing decline of both accumulated gains and principal, with punishing surrender charges standing between the investor and a hasty retreat from further loss.

Let's say you have a $12,000 variable annuity and during the first year of the contract, you decide to withdraw $6,000, or half the value of the entire annuity. Like most annuity contracts, you are allowed to take out up to 10 percent per year without penalty, which means that you would not pay a surrender penalty on $1,200 of the $6,000 you withdrew. You would be charged a penalty on the remaining $4,800, and with some annuities charging 10 percent or more for early withdrawals during the first contract year, you would pay $480, or more, for the withdrawal of the $4,800.

With the variable annuity, you might also face **mortality/expense-risk (MER) charges**, which equate to a specific percentage of the total value of an annuity account. This fee, often around 1.25 percent, is charged each year by the insurance carrier to cover risks associated with the annuity. As opposed to market risk, the insurance company's actual risk is more like the cost of selling the annuity. The MER charge helps offset the cost of the original sales commission the company paid the annuity salesperson who sold you the variable annuity.

If the MER fee appears nominal to you at first glance, consider this: a $20,000 annuity facing a 1.25 percent annual MER fee means that $250 comes out of the contract account each year. If you take out half of this account, or $10,000, and the contract imposes a 10 percent annual cap on withdrawals, you would not be charged for $2,000 of the total withdrawal, but you would take a hit on the remaining $8,000. Given a 10 percent surrender charge, you would pay $800 plus the $250 MER charge, for a total of $1,050.

Next are the **underlying fund expenses**, which you pay through the insurance company to the mutual-fund managers who handle the investments purchased on your behalf by the insurance company. In that arena, you might also find fees for **sales loads**, which are otherwise known as trading fees. Sales loads, which are commonplace in the industry, are charged when parts of your account are transferred to and from various investments.

The trail of fees may also include **administrative charges**. These are fees for items such as data management and other expenses, and they may be charged as flat fees—with or without early withdrawals. This charge is often listed in a variable annuity contract as being based on a percentage (around 0.15 percent annually) of your total account value. In such a case, your administrative fees grow with the value of your variable annuity account, with a $20,000 account generating $30 in annual fees.

Such fees are often found on a list in the variable annuity's pro-spectus and should be considered alongside the annuity's benefits, such as the **guaranteed minimum income benefit,** a **long-term care (LTC) insurance** rider, and/or the **stepped-up death bene-fit**—some or all of which may be offered by the variable annuity provider. For more about variable annuity fees and other details, visit www.sec.gov, which was also the source for some of the preced-ing information.

Sorting Out the Differences

In general, annuities offer advantages over other retirement ve-hicles, including CDs and mutual funds. For one, all fixed annuities guarantee principal, so you never lose money if you follow the terms of the contract. With a variety of fixed annuities, you receive steady returns. And as the value of the fixed annuity grows, the growth continues free of income taxes, allowing for the compounding ac-cumulation of value and tax-advantaged growth. However, with a variable annuity, your returns remain uncertain or flat for periods of time, thus fueling the argument that they freeze assets that could be overtaken by inflation.

Fixed and fixed-indexed annuities also allow for cash withdraw-als from time to time, but only after specified periods of time and in limited quantities. This is part of the power of the annuity, of course—the holder must allow the annuity to accumulate value. If you want complete access to your money at all times, put it in the bank, where growth rates have been slim to none and trail behind the rate of inflation.

Another nice feature of fixed and fixed-indexed annuities is that your principal remains untouched by fees and commissions. Annui-ties also carry provisions providing for a lifetime of guaranteed in-come with additional tax advantages. Yet one of the more valuable qualities of the annuity is often forgotten until it really counts: if the annuitant, or annuity holder, dies, his or her principal and proceeds can automatically go to designated heirs, thus avoiding probate de-lays and expenses. Challenges to the estate of the deceased are not possible if proceeds are held in annuities with named beneficiaries.

I use fixed-indexed annuities that go a bit further—the ones I use are tied to positive changes in the S&P 500 to capture any increases, *but none of the losses*. If you were to invest in one of my selected fixed-indexed annuities this year and the S&P gained 10 percent, your annuity's value may increase 6 to 7 percent. Every cent of the 6 to 7 percent gain becomes principal, which is safely tucked away for the future. And if the S&P loses 10 percent the following year, your annuity loses no value. You can't lose, but you won't gain anything that year.

What, no gain? No, but let's be reasonable. If you had the same money in a mutual fund tied to the S&P, you would capture the full 10 percent increase in the first year. But you would also shoulder the full 10 percent loss the following year, plus a portion of your principal through management fees and/or commissions.

There are various formulas for indexing, depending on how the company credits the interest. The formulas vary from company to company and are too numerous to review here, but the key is to understand how the one you are using works. This is where a good safe-retirement advocate comes in, because, in the long run, all formulas are designed to give similar results depending on market conditions. The real key is the quality of the company and the company's renewal history. You need a good advocate to help you in this area.

You, Basic Math, and Retirement Reality

You may find my own personal story somewhat ironic, but let me explain who I am. I got my start in academia as a mathematician. The financial planning field came naturally to me because mathematical probabilities play an important role in good financial planning. You might even say that certain aspects of successful retirement planning methodologies are fundamentally "academic" in the mathematical sense, and this alone might help you qualify your choice of financial advisors.

So why did I face a personal dilemma when planning my *own* retirement? Some people get a chuckle out of this, but it's because retirement planning means more than just mathematical probabilities.

When I tried to logically evaluate my own retirement, I looked at the hard facts of my future income needs in retirement (the math), and then factored the more subjective wants of my own "dream" scenario (the emotions) to construct the perfect retirement lifestyle. The sum total of that process left me distraught because I wanted so many things, such as the freedom to travel and pursue new hobbies.

With my own emotional complexities interwoven into mathematical probabilities, I suppose I lacked the objectivity of a qualified, third-party financial advisor. I basically confused myself in the initial, emotionally charged process of self-discovery until I found the practical and emotional bottom line. Like most people, I ultimately wanted the guaranteed peace of mind of an absolutely secure retirement plan.

From there, the rest was easy. Every mathematical model led to the same conclusion: I could not avoid the fact that certain income needs required a guaranteed income stream. Regardless of the given risk tolerance of any investment (high, low, or in between), risk is risk. In order to find true peace of mind, I found the need for a bedrock guarantee of income for the basics: health care, household expenses, and proper nutrition, just to name a few. That was my experience. Now, let's talk about yours.

Try to absolutely guarantee income for basic necessities, and you will quickly rule out any kind of dependence on risk-related financial instruments. At certain points in our lives, on the other hand, we may find it too risky to proceed without a certain element of risk-associated instruments in the marketplace. So where do you find the best of both worlds? One, you need to avoid risk altogether to ensure funds for the necessities of a lifetime in retirement. Two, when evaluating financial instruments associated with the marketplace, do the math and you will always seem to arrive at the same fundamental equation. Trust me. It's always the same: risk-free necessities + care-free retirement = annuities.

There's no way around it: Annuities have to play some role—most likely a fundamental role for many of us—in our retirement plans. After all, insurance companies offer annuities. Annuities are basically insurance contracts that guarantee your principal, which makes perfect sense: you need to look for an insurance policy for your money.

After a lot of research, I discovered that quality annuities are some of the best instruments out there for retirement security. Good annuities offer enough gain to offset inflation—again, with principal guaranteed—and they provide an income stream to cover some of the basics, guaranteed.

At the risk of oversimplifying things, an annuity is an insurance contract. The contract guarantees an income stream you cannot outlive. When properly structured among other assets in your portfolio, the annuity will be a boon for covering expenses you cannot live without. Without an annuity, you may run into trouble; I've seen it happen so many times before. Social Security and pension payouts were supposed to cover the essentials, but after suffering the combined abuses of growing inflation, escalating prescription-drug costs, and the unpredictable ways taxes eat into Social Security payments and Medicare and Medicaid stipends, most have seen a need to fill the gap.

An annuity is the best way to fill that gap. At some point, every one of us will need additional income in our financial future. Because we'll need it most when we find ourselves beyond our earning years, that crucial "gap" income must be ensured. What better way to ensure that income than through an insurance instrument for your money? There is no better way, and the fixed annuity is one such instrument.

An elite few are fortunate enough to have a vast arsenal of assets. They will be able to spend unlimited amounts of money for the rest of their lives and can afford to take risks on the purchase of anything from gold futures to highly speculative securities offerings. If they win, they win. If they lose, who cares? How could they relate to the 99.9 percent of us who make up the rest of this country, who very possibly will exhaust every source of income before we die?

As safe-retirement advocates, my colleagues and I have studied most forms of threat to income; unfortunately, our studies continue every day because new threats continue to surface. Every time Congress restructures the tax code, for example, we find ourselves scrambling to reengineer our asset-planning strategies.

When this happens, you will—with any luck—be working with an honest, competent financial planner, a fully qualified safe-retirement advocate. Unfortunately, the field is full of incompetence and, in some rare cases, outright fraud. At best, inexperienced planners often leave their clients with unrealistic expectations. At worst, they fail to adequately account for the short-term volatility of market returns and the probability of inflation.

While we have fairly precise mathematical models at our disposal and the ability to apply our clients' portfolios to these models, many in the planning field may not be aware of them, or they may lack the expertise to apply them. But even financial professionals working with the best mathematical probability models are no substitute for professionals with direct experience. Only decades of experience in the financial services field give financial planners the tools to deal with people who have already fallen victim to income threats. By the time these people come to me for emergency repair of their retirement plans, many have run so low on money they have been forced to return to work. Some have already become financially dependent upon their own children for support.

No wonder so many of us today live in fear of running out of money in retirement. Too many times, I've faced people in need of emergency repairs after spending years working with an incompetent financial planner. At that point, there was little I could do for them. I had no easy answer for people who had been fed the "greed scenario" to the point of bankruptcy. They'd followed the advice of consultants who had ignored safe-haven savings plans and instead favored risk over common sense.

That kind of experience is sad and frustrating for those of us with enough experience to value safe-retirement planning. A truly qualified professional knows it is so very simple to eliminate the most commonly known threats to a secure retirement. We've already talked about the threats, so let's examine the cure, which first requires an examination of public perception. In my opinion, there are two basic types of perception—those based on experience and those based on hearsay. We have a definite problem with the latter.

To battle hearsay, experience will eventually compel people like me to act as fierce advocates for safe-retirement planning. For me, this kind of advocacy is part of my daily routine. I write letters and make phone calls to insurance providers and politicians, all in an effort to drive improvements in products and services. Did I fail to mention that not all annuities are perfect? You should be hearing this from any competent annuity representative. Some annuities are so poorly structured that they pose risk rather than sanctuary for your principal.

Before we get into that, you need to know about a certain ongoing situation, the propagation of disinformation. I've said this directly to media people, politicians, and anyone of influence who will listen: to better understand the value of a *quality* annuity, you need to know one when you see it. From there, we can better understand the critical value of a solid annuity as a fundamental cornerstone of retirement planning. Unfortunately, shoddy annuities get a lot of publicity, and most of it is sensationalized and inaccurate.

I continue to stress the need to understand quality annuities, because frankly, the industry faces a well-orchestrated battle for the attention of incoming baby-boom retirees. As such, competing financial entities outside the annuity industry have fueled a new breed of criticism, much of which is highly speculative criticism based on pure hearsay. This criticism seeks to undermine annuities overall. Why? To ultimately promote the sale of risk-bearing investments, of course. The promoters of such instruments want to keep all the marbles for themselves—and we know who they are. Yet if some judiciously represent the necessary risk portion of a portfolio, others tout the possibility of outlandishly unrealistic returns. As a result, people get burned.

You should also know that the battle between annuities and securities will continue because certain interests want safe-haven cash-insurance instruments like annuities to disappear altogether. Therefore, they will continue to undermine the legitimacy of the annuity, which has been with us since the days of ancient Rome.

The anti-annuity message is often subtle, accepting some aspects of annuities while condemning others. Some of this criticism arises from real experiences with the very few annuities that actually are leveraged in favor of providers and unscrupulous salespeople. While you need to know what those annuities are and where they come from, the mixed message coming from most media today is seriously tainted by sources from a competing industry—securities. The net effect is a sudden and vaguely unfavorable impression of annuities among certain consumers. After all, they've heard it time and again from the get-rich sector led by certain financial-risk promoters.

That type of so-called advisor is, by the way, a fast-fading minority. I've seen more and more reputable Wall Street analysts take center stage since the 2001 crash, and these folks are not opposed to guaranteed income. They see fixed annuities as necessary components of most retirement portfolios.

Yet for many people planning retirement, the damage has already been done. Because of this relentless anti-annuity message, the very people who could benefit most from annuities tend to avoid them—the hallmark of an upcoming tragedy yet to unfold. Without the foundation of a solid fixed annuity and other savings instruments, a generation of incoming retirees is bound to revisit the bitter lessons of the 2001 market crash and the 2007–2008 meltdown of the overall financial sector. Mark my words: the irony will come with a period of renewed optimism, which will be followed by another downturn. Unless annuity advocates can turn the message back to center, the moment we all see an upward market, we'll once again be lulled into complacency by the siren song of the "go-go-can't-lose" mentality of the late 1990s.

Taking on the Critics

In order to turn the tide of strategic messaging from the anti-annuity camp, let's take a hard look at the fuel of this criticism, much of which comes from certain company-leveraged annuity products that dump excessive fees on consumers. These kinds of questionable annuities also carry steep surrender charges and excessive surrender periods.

A surrender charge is a fee charged to the owner of an annuity if she decides to terminate the annuity and withdraw principal and proceeds before the annuity matures. If an owner decides to cash out of a ten-year annuity early, before the full maturity period has transpired, surrender charges kick in, and they can be quite steep. Such charges would be highest—perhaps 10 to 15 percent of principal and accumulated value—during the first year of the annuity contract and would steadily decline to the lowest level, perhaps 1 percent, during the tenth and final year of the annuity.

Of all the criticisms of annuities that have surfaced in recent years, surrender charges for early withdrawal seem to head the list. Media come at this from one basic angle, and rightfully so. Surrender charges can be excessive, and I have long advocated a more consumer-friendly fee structure. Yet the more aggravating aspect of the surrender-charge issue lies directly at the doorstep of the annuity salesperson who fails to fully explain the surrender charges to the client. That same salesperson might not mention that many annuity products offer a mitigating bonus that is built into the product and can counteract the impact of the surrender charge.

A **bonus product**, or an annuity product that offers a bonus as an incentive to purchase it, essentially offers the annuity buyer a cash bonus to be added to the buyer's initial principal contribution to the annuity. If, for example, a buyer contributes $100,000 to an annuity and the signing bonus from the annuity provider is 10 percent, the buyer's annuity account might begin with $110,000 and grow from there. However, some annuity contracts may require annuity buyers to remain with the contract until it matures in order to collect the bonus.

Other bonus annuities might offer consumers an enticing upfront cash bonus, but the tradeoff could be unusually high surrender charges for early withdrawal that offset the cost of the bonus to the annuity company. Such annuities could also be structured to make it easier for the company to take back the bonus if the buyer opts for early withdrawal. A prudent planner rarely, if ever, uses large bonus products to offset high surrender charges when setting up annuities because, more often than not, annuities with high surrender charges are also annuities with high bonuses and contractual technicalities attached. Prudent planners look for a variety of flexible annuity features based on the individual needs of each client.

Surrender charges do serve a function, however. As with other financial products, they encourage a commitment to a long-term strategy because the insurance carrier must also commit to a long-term strategy in order to grow your principal contribution. It works the same way with other financial instruments as well. This is basically a long-term savings strategy with nicely built-in earnings along the way.

Bank CDs also offer savings strategies, but without the level of increase offered by annuities. As a result, their fees for early withdrawal tend to be lower. And financial investment products like mutual funds ask for a long-term commitment to investment strategies, so they similarly impose penalties for early withdrawal, which in some cases can be hefty as well.

With annuities, early withdrawal will cost you, no matter how you cut the pie. For that reason, enter into a contract for any form of savings instrument or investment with that in mind. If you have only $10,000 to your name, with no other recourse for medical and other emergencies, why would you sink every penny of it into a savings tool like an annuity, mutual fund, or some other instrument, all with back-end penalties for early withdrawal?

Financial "planning" means just that: to plan by looking at the big picture and diversify according to both your visible goals *and* the unforeseen. That said, let's take a hard look at surrender charges, the method behind the mayhem, and the actual value the charges present to a well-crafted retirement plan.

At one point in the past, a particular insurance carrier offered an annuity product, which, if properly applied, would work well for many different kinds of clients. This product—like many other annuities—imposed a first-year surrender charge of 18 percent of the buyer's "excessive withdrawal" of an amount over the allowable

10 percent yearly withdrawal, meaning 18 percent of the amount of money withdrawn in excess of the already permitted annual withdrawal of 10 percent. At the time, this product also offered an immediate bonus equal to 10 percent of the premium, so the 18 percent surrender charge really amounted to an 8 percent penalty against the buyer's principal if the contract were terminated in the first year.

Most, if not all, annuities offer an allowable penalty-free annual withdrawal of cash for emergencies, mad money—whatever. It's your money, up to a point. But as outlined elsewhere in this book, the insurance company selling the annuity uses your contribution to buy things, such as bonds, for which you get a guaranteed return, regardless of the actual risk assumed by the insurance company. The obvious upshot here is that when you back out of the deal early on, the insurance company is forced to assume a greater risk of exposure. Surrender charges are imposed to discourage the latter and to absorb costs. Truth be told, some surrender charges *are* unwarranted. Some companies impose excessive surrender charges but still offer escape-valve withdrawal features, such as a very necessary medical emergency/nursing-home withdrawal allowance.

We'll cover all that later, but for now, simply remember that this particular contract decreased from a surrender charge of 18 percent (offset by the 10 percent bonus) in the first year to 16 percent the second year, eventually winding down to 2 percent during the final year of the ten-year annuity. While other features probably offered balancing factors for the buyer, a typical annuity contract should clearly reference the surrender charges of the annuity. Annuity contracts vary in size from 30 to 120 pages, so ask your advisor to review the contract with you to ensure that you completely understand these figures.

You should also know that an 18 percent surrender charge (again, offset by the 10 percent bonus) is not necessarily out of line in this industry. Another product may start with a first-year surrender charge of 16 percent and decline over a ten-year period to 4 percent. Yet another may have a surrender charge of 15 percent for the first four years that drops to 2.1 percent in year ten. All of these options suggest that such charges are to be expected, although different companies offer all sorts of products with different surrender charges—some high, some low, and some with features designed to offset surrender charge rates.

Reliable companies typically balance such charges with an array of features and cost-saving alternatives, and certain states, including Connecticut, Delaware, and Pennsylvania, actually mandate lower surrender charges by law. Be sure to ask for a brochure about any annuity product you are considering, because it should disclose surrender information as well as any variations mandated by the state.

So you know that surrender charges vary widely. You also know what to expect in terms of industry standards, which may very well inspire more timely disclosure from your annuity salesperson. Given the hard numbers that should be available during any annuity sales presentation, you should be able to have a productive discussion about mitigating or balancing the pros and cons of various options, including the offsetting features of each annuity. Low surrender fees may be offered for a reason—such as limited early-withdrawal features and bonuses.

The bottom line is that annuities can be highly productive, wealth-preserving forms of guaranteed income when you need it most. However, they are essentially savings instruments, often with a costly lock on the piggy bank during the early years of accumulation. They should be considered accordingly and put in the proper perspective. While any good financial planner would tell you this, a true safe-retirement advocate will go into considerable detail about them, providing facts and figures for all of the aforementioned, including every feature that offsets or balances surrender charges and other related issues.

Some annuity buyers are never told, for example, about options like the **walk-away premium bonus**, which can be 10 percent or more added to one's original principal. This type of bonus is typically offered by an annuity provider upon the annuity's purchase; it may come guaranteed, regardless of whether or not a customer stays with the contract. Such a bonus could be used to reduce the impact of a larger first-year surrender charge.

The industry is constantly evolving to make such consumer-friendly products. For example, some insurance carriers offer annuity contracts with a **return-of-premium feature**. If at any time you are unhappy with the annuity, the insurance carrier will refund your total premium. (Keep in mind, however, that you will have to forfeit any bonus or earned interest to do so.)

An even greater danger for the consumer comes from unscrupulous annuity salespeople who seek high commissions. The salesperson's motive may be purely monetary, and such salespeople may not always put their clients' needs first.

We'll talk later about how commissions work in the annuity contract, but first, let's cover the commission-inspired sale of annuities and what you may *not* hear about in a sales presentation. First, salespeople rarely reveal the commission they receive from the sale of an annuity, nor are commissions mentioned in standard annuity contracts. But the motivation to earn the commission may drive some salespeople to err by omission. They may lack the overall competence, training, and expertise to properly apply an annuity to a complete financial planning strategy because some of these people may have been trained with a sole focus on maximizing their sales and their own earnings. Of course, such people need to either leave the business or get more education, because their efforts taint an entire industry.

The bottom line: Ask your salesperson to list comparative surrender fees and periods for annuities other than the one being presented. Other products should compare favorably, or at least competitively, to the one suggested by your annuity representative. Also, look for some of the following features and bonus packages as a benchmark when considering any annuity.

*1. Products offering 5 percent and 10 percent **signing bonuses** are not uncommon in this industry.* Some may come guaranteed from the first year onward, meaning they can help offset a future surrender charge, and others require that contract-holders avoid withdrawals for the length of the annuity before cashing in on the bonus. Still others may allow for a fully vested bonus to be received after a portion of the accumulation period has passed—say, ten years into a fifteen-year annuity.

*2. Ask if any of the above arrangements come with other **no-fee withdrawal allowances**.* Most companies let contract holders withdraw at least 10 percent of principal in any given year, which is not a gift but a competitive standard. A 10 percent penalty-free withdrawal per year is a fairly standard feature in most annuity contracts. However, some annuity salespeople may make it sound as if you're getting a gift or a special feature if the contract they're discussing includes this important item. Don't believe it: you should expect an annual 10 percent withdrawal allowance.

Some annuities also build in additional death benefits for surviving beneficiaries, while most include a **nursing-home rider**, which is an allowance for additional withdrawals for unexpected nursing-home expenses. Certain nursing-home riders even allow an additional 10 percent annual withdrawal or more, should such medical emergencies occur, but you must look carefully at the contract's fine print. If one contract's nursing-home rider allows an additional 20 percent annual withdrawal, it may require a waiting period of a year or two after the contract's purchase. The same rider might also require that the contract owner be confined to a nursing home for 90 to 120 days or more before the rider can take effect, and additional nursing-home rider fees may or may not be imposed—all of which should be clearly outlined in the contract.

If the annuity policyholder is in a nursing home for more than sixty days in a row, some nursing-home riders forgive all surrender fees after the first year of purchase. Another 100 percent surrender-charge waiver might come in the form of a **terminal-illness rider** if the annuity owner has been advised that she has less than a year to live.

Some annuities additionally offer **unemployment riders**, giving annuity owners penalty-free access to principal if they are under age sixty-five and have been unemployed for more than thirty consecutive days.

3. *You might also ask about the presence of a **market-value adjustment (MVA)** in a proposed annuity contract.* The MVA basically allows an annuity owner to share the risk of his or her own early surrender prior to the contract's date of maturity. While formulas vary, the MVA triggers an increase in the **surrender value** (monies exposed to surrender charges, that is) as overall market interest rates fall during various economic conditions. The upside is that your

surrender values fall as prevailing interest rates rise. Therefore, in terms of your latitude in controlling potential surrender charges, an MVA may or may not be a good thing.

I favor fixed annuity products overall, so naturally I favor a predictable, fixed schedule of surrender charges. In general, I advise clients to shop around to find a product that allows a surrender-charge schedule they can afford. Such a search should be done during the initial stage of retirement planning, as you consider all of your cash, investments, savings, and other financial resources.

Could an MVA cause the value of your fixed annuity to actually sink below the original value of your principal? Not on my watch— nor have I ever heard of such a thing occurring with reliable fixed annuities. The only ways in which your principal contribution may be vulnerable are if you end an annuity contract early, before interest earnings have had a chance to accumulate, or if your annual withdrawals exceed allowable limits.

Details abound from there. As in any industry, some products are better designed and more efficient than others. Such products tend to be represented and sold by people with more experience and training, and these people also are usually better educated and show greater concern for their clients. Experience drives the bus in this arena, because experienced professionals know the value of selling quality over quantity, and accordingly, they see far fewer problems. They receive compliments and referrals from customers, rather than complaints. They know from experience that presenting a quality annuity is the best route to building a business in this industry. Unfortunately, not all annuity reps see it the same way.

Some of these ethically challenged annuity reps may forget to mention part of the downsides that you may hesitate to ask about, particularly when it comes to annuities with low surrender charges. There's no free lunch, right? If a fixed annuity offers a suspiciously low surrender charge, it may lack access to a **premium bonus** if surrender charges are triggered in any way.

To put it another way, you may not get the premium bonus if you fail to stick with the annuity through the entire maturity period. For example, if the annuity has a suspiciously low surrender charge, check the fine print, because early withdrawal might trigger more than just the surrender charge. With this type of annuity, activation of the surrender charge might also cause you to lose access to any bonus originally offered by the provider. This loss of access essentially cancels the bonus. Meanwhile, other annuities with higher surrender charges might allow you to keep the bonus if you withdraw early (or at nearly any point in time with some products), which could be used to offset the surrender charge.

If some annuities allow owners to begin withdrawing the additional accumulated value of an annuity, this might be used as a selling point, but ask for specifics: for example, certain annuities restrict such withdrawals until the contract has been in force for at least five years of a ten-year maturity period. Also, if the annuity charges a low, or no-fee, penalty for this feature, access to the contract's accumulation value does not necessarily equate to full access to the account.

Other caveats include basically poor features that leave the consumer at risk in terms of good financial planning. To get to the bottom of these, let's take a closer look at a particular annuity that offers lower surrender charges. As with other annuities, the principal is always guaranteed with this stable, fixed annuity, but unlike others in its class, it offers little more than 3 percent compounded annual interest as a minimum guarantee. This is a worst-case scenario that stands a good chance of falling behind inflation growth rates. In addition, this particular annuity doesn't even offer so much as a modest signing bonus! However, this may not necessarily be a bad thing for certain people. If you're offering 3 percent minimum compounding interest in addition to a chance of greater returns, sign me up—but I'm only willing to take lower compounding interest guarantees in return for greater potential interest credits.

Such a balanced presentation of features may not fit a particular agent's sales objectives, and that may lead to problems. Salespeople who are blind to real customer needs and their clients' welfare tend to be in it for the short haul and the fast buck; they're busy planning their own early retirements after accruing ill-gotten means from their shoddy annuities.

Fortunately for my clients, and the clients of my colleagues in the Quiet Revolution, qualified annuity professionals love to study, and in particular we love to study the subject of annuities. We're always looking for the latest innovations, regulations, legislation, methodology, features, and applications involving annuities. Much of this comes from continuing education, but I also like to test and retest my own mathematical models, constantly updating them with my past experiences to meet current and future realities in the economy.

Thankfully, I am not alone in this arena. There are other financial professionals like me. Our numbers are growing. You need not stand—or sit—still for the fast-buck artist I mentioned earlier. I've given you some ways to recognize these individuals and some questions that might help you weed them out, but you're the one in the driver's seat. You have to ask the questions. This is where *you* come in.

Here's another way to separate the pros from the run-of-the-mill (or worse) annuity professionals. To be really successful in this business, a planner has to love the technicalities, the details, the economics, and the people-driven details of the process. That's where customer satisfaction comes from. When you sit down with a true professional, you will recognize the difference almost immediately. We never scramble for answers to complex questions because we have lived them first hand. We often know the depth and detail of upcoming legislation that applies to retirement planning well before it hits the financial press. The annuity products we represent have been similarly researched in every detail and are carefully chosen to precisely integrate into a client's overall financial plan.

Some people call what I've just described an expression of character and evidence of responsibility. That's fine, but I believe those professional qualities are essential to the establishment of long-term relationships and the very nature of success in our business. You should expect that kind of dedication from your planner. Solid relationships with clients and with quality insurance providers are at the heart of building a dependable business. Therefore, reputable planners always work hard to build relationships with those insurance companies that have demonstrated a commitment to **consumer-leveraged**

products and services, which are any products that are advantageous to consumers. Consumer-leveraged annuity products are structured in the consumer's best interest, as opposed to the self-serving interest of the provider. Consumer-leveraged products are entering the annuity marketplace at a faster pace than ever before.

It should not be surprising that the companies offering these products are among the most financially secure in the world. They offer products with lower fees, better returns, and greater flexibility for the consumer, and they've been around for a long time. You just need to know who they are. An experienced, ethical annuity consultant will tell you, but an inexperienced, unscrupulous salesperson may not. Always remember your responsibility to ask questions about the annuities you're considering, and don't forget to ask specific questions about ratings provided by **insurance-industry rating services**, such as A.M. Best. Also remember that any guarantees with an annuity are contingent upon the claims-paying ability of the insurance company.

If an annuity representative can't seem to locate the rating of the annuity he's trying to sell you, you might consider locating another representative.

CHAPTER 3

Separating the Wheat from the Chaff:
Planners Good and Evil Exposed

A
S YOU SELECT A FINANCIAL PLANNER, THE FIRST CHALLENGE IS the question-and-answer process. If you find yourself dealing with someone who jumps to conclusions without asking lots of questions, beware.

People with my level of experience are unique in the field of annuities. (I have firsthand sensitivity for the concerns of today's retiree, since I'm nearing that age myself.) Over the years, we've experienced many triumphs of good planning, and we've witnessed the woes that have befallen clients with poor strategies from other planners. To avoid the latter, we have spent years drafting and redrafting precisely crafted questions to frame the concerns of incoming clients.

If a planner fails to ask a few hard questions, be skeptical. Planners must ask detailed questions because they need the numbers to analyze your financial condition. I need to probe every detail of your financial life to assess your income, your asset types and asset performance, your investment style, and your risk tolerance. I do *not* need that information to sell you more investments; instead, I need that information to recommend the best annuity products to guarantee you income should your other assets fail to perform. This is my job, and my job requires candor. I am not trying to win a popularity contest, and not everyone will accept my advice, but those clients who do are pleased with the results because they know the relief of having a secure retirement.

The bottom line is that come what may in the stock market, annuities will always be there. Your income will continue regardless of the myriad factors that can and will adversely affect the regional, national, and global economy.

Unfortunately, I've got something big going against me: the ever-present label of "salesperson." For all our mathematical computations, risk-assessment modeling, financial analysis, and other factors that are required of an ethical practitioner, people with my level of experience are still sometimes dubbed salespeople, just like everyone else in the industry. But unlike someone selling furniture, cars, or jewelry, I stay in business only if my sales fit the appropriate context of a complex financial scenario, which should include a strategic mix of other investments and legal instruments orchestrated by a team of skilled professionals.

If you find yourself in the company of someone who seems to be familiar with only one or two annuity product lines, you are likely dealing with an inexperienced annuity salesperson, as opposed to a financial planning professional. These people may get in and out of the deal, dance off with a commission, and leave behind more questions than answers.

If people with true expertise have a major weakness, it's taking on too much responsibility for a client's financial well being. If we believe that a client has invested too much in risk-bearing assets, such as stocks and bonds, we'll create charts and tables to prove it. If the client still rejects the analysis, we can't just live with the rejection and move on, which is a typical sales mentality. Instead, we spend hours analyzing our own failure to communicate. I've redrafted long-term asset performance histories and reexamined my interview process countless times, knowing that I sometimes take more time than most to really understand a client's needs.

On the other hand, I realize that I am dealing with a conservative product. An annuity will never make you a quick million overnight. Anyone who says otherwise and tries to fill your asset portfolio with nothing but annuities falls—in my humble opinion—into the category of the snake-oil salesperson. In fact, a writer for a major consumer magazine once put it exactly that way when referring to the sales tactics of certain unethical individuals and annuity products.

That kind of person and product is by far a minority in this business. If certain media people really think they've uncovered these hucksters for the first time, they should get real. Most of us at the leading edge of advocacy in this industry have worked long and hard to eradicate this "snake-oil" level of misrepresentation and consumer-hostile product design. As a result, hucksters and their snake-oil products seldom last long, but you do need to be aware of them.

What's Right for You?

Next, let's look at the upside of guaranteed-income planning. Finding the best annuity option is dependent on individual needs and situations. Conventional wisdom obviously calls for an annuity contract to offer the essential guarantees of income planning, and in this regard, the industry has added major innovations to empower the real purpose of the annuity, which is to provide guarantees and future income.

The income-seeking client. Advisors have been wishing and waiting for **guaranteed lifetime-income withdrawal benefits** for years, and they're finally here. This benefit, acquired by the purchase of a rider, can cost between 0 and 0.5 percent of the buyer's account value. It dictates that an account used solely for income will grow at a specific percentage rate, compounded, until the consumer elects to begin receiving income. The client is then guaranteed a fixed income, which can never decrease, for as long as she lives. As the client receives the income, which is deducted from the account each year, the remaining balance may still earn credits, allowing the account to grow at the same time. Many carriers now offer these outstanding riders, and some are available at no charge. Others impose only a modest fee (up to 0.50 percent of the account value) on an annual basis and leave the basic annuity contract unchanged. Accumulated values are still credited the same exact way, as if no rider had been attached, and the rider creates another "balance" for income purposes.

Combined with your original premium (plus applicable bonuses), this additional "balance" allows the annuity to grow at a compounded guaranteed rate of as much as 8 percent per year until you start your income stream. When you are ready to begin receiving income, your payments will be based on the higher figure of your actual accumulated value—the **guaranteed growth value**—which will determine the amount to be paid out to you for the rest of your life. Based on your age at the time the income stream begins, this income can never be outgrown.

The difference between this type of income payment and traditional annuity income streams is that after a payment has been made, the balance of your annuity will still be earning **index credits**. Therefore, you have growth in your annuity during both the accumulation and distribution phases of your contract.

The safe harbor–seeking client. If you are not looking for income and instead just want to guarantee the safety of your money, you may seek an annuity with the lowest surrender charges available and a good mix of premium bonuses and other consumer-friendly features, including generous nursing-home riders. When planning for this type of client, I tend to look for an immediate 10 percent signing bonus and as much safety as I can get. Some annuities might offer **mixed allocation** as well, which means that your money can be allocated to (or applied to) a mixed variety of earning methods. For example, such products might allow a significant portion of the annuity to lock into a guaranteed 3 to 4 percent annual growth rate while letting the remaining portion participate in some sort of index activity, like the S&P 500. As of this writing, several such products offered upside potential of 5 to 7 percent on the index side of the annuity, without exposing principal and accumulated interest to downside risk.

However, such products sometimes come with stiff surrender charges in exchange for great bonuses. Buyers should not buy these products if they have any possibility of needing access to the account before it matures into a lump-sum distribution or income payout. Annuities are long-term, tax-deferred, income planning vehicles, and if you are looking for a place to put your money away until you are ready to receive a guaranteed income stream, look no further. I will continue to stress the importance of this issue and urge you to speak to your advisor openly and honestly about your finances in order to ensure that you find the product that best fits your goals.

The flexible client. Some clients have considerable flexibility in their long-term retirement plans. When I am serving such a client's needs, I look for flexibility with guaranteed growth. Some index annuities with a mixed allocation provide at least 1 percent of additional credit on the index activity side of the mix, even when all the market indices are in the tank. To obtain that kind of guarantee, however, you may be looking at a high-end growth limitation of 6 to 7 percent of your total account value, along with the aforementioned 1 percent growth attached to the original principal. Remember, that's the whole purpose of an indexed annuity—modest growth with downside protection! You won't have to watch and worry that your balance will fluctuate with unfavorable market conditions.

If you have enough flexibility in your overall retirement portfolio for periods of flat growth—again, with no risk to principal—you might consider certain **nonbonus products** if they offer a significantly higher ceiling of upside market potential. For example, some annuities offer more adventurous buyers the upside potential of up to 9.8 percent in annual interest credits based on point-to-point activity on the S&P 500. Insurance providers can afford to promise guarantees like this because they are taking on no risk in the form of a bonus, and because providers and annuity owners are essentially equally vested in the annuity contract. As a result, this type of product also carries relatively low surrender charges.

Really Getting to Know Clients and Networking with Other Providers

Because financial planning in general, and annuity products in particular, are widely misunderstood, I sometimes get a little desperate and try to cram too much into my first encounter with a potential client. We all know the fundamentals of purchasing a home or car, each of which has its own complexities. Likewise, each part of your financial plan must be carefully integrated with other highly complex instruments.

Imagine trying to buy a house based on the integrated complexities of a car you currently own. What if the garage had to support the precise mechanical aspects of your car? Suppose the kitchen had to be geometrically aligned with the upstairs study in order for the appliances to operate? That level of integration is sometimes needed in the financial planning process, so your planner must have enough knowledge and professional respect to deal with a host of other professionals.

On a daily basis, I'm in contact with certified public accountants, estate attorneys, securities brokers, and insurance providers. On behalf of some of my clients, I deal with bankers, mortgage brokers, and even family psychologists from time to time. It takes a high degree of confidence and expertise to hold your own with that crowd, so if you find your planner is at all hesitant to speak with others on your financial team, you should wonder about his qualifications.

Because truly experienced financial professionals know how to interact with the greater financial universe, I truly believe that our products and services are the best solutions for our clients, and this level of confidence can be important in times of economic crisis. You'll know a real professional because her knowledge-driven calm in a chaotic economic environment will shine through. We've been there often enough to avoid panic, and we've learned to be quick on our feet when called upon to act during periods of financial upheaval.

We've also learned to teach in a classroom setting without being pedantic or condescending. Good planners' financial workshops are strictly informational, framed for training prospective clients about the fundamentals of retirement planning without dwelling upon specific annuity products.

I also train other financial professionals on behalf of a national network of financial planners. After decades in the business, I am able to train both clients and planners because I know my subject well. I love what I do, and I know I can rely on the annuity products I represent. This confidence is essential to the process of annuity presentation and sales. A professional must know his subject inside and out, and he must use blunt honesty and personal experiences to discuss the pros and cons of annuities in given situations. Experienced planners only provide carefully detailed facts, allowing clients to make up their own minds about the products they recommend.

This is the critical difference: you will never find seasoned planners pressing for a sale. It just doesn't work that way. When dealing with numbers (I am definitely a numbers person) it takes time and incremental presentation to allow data to sink in. At the same time, good planners have little time for an unctuous, patronizing approach to sales. Instead, good planners are very good listeners. They need to hear what you have to say—otherwise, how could they possibly integrate their own recommendations into the complex process of retirement planning and ultimately earn your trust?

The first sign of a good listener is an ability to ask pertinent questions that directly relate to your financial future. These may be questions of a personal nature—for example, the treatment of potential heirs. Your financial planner needs to know about your own personal, and sometimes emotional, needs to identify which financial issues matter most to you.

On the road to becoming mathematically analytical and emotionally empathetic, your planner should assess your comfort level when dealing with the math involved in retirement planning and tailor your planning sessions accordingly. For example, if you have little patience for statistical charts and tables, the planner can pare the numbers down to analytical essentials given to you in digestible increments, so you can absorb the information over a period of time. When the planner presents information related to the emotionally essential components of your lifestyle, you should feel the meaning of the numbers as they relate to you, your family, and the future you envision for yourself. This takes considerable skill developed over many years, but in the end, it allows seasoned professionals to apply mathematical principles to real-life situations so virtually any client can understand she needs to know.

If you haven't seen some—or all—of these qualities in your financial planner, you should get a second opinion about your retirement plan. It's critical that you thoroughly understand every detail of any plan, annuity, or financial instrument you intend to purchase before you sign on the dotted line. If you feel rushed, pressured, or—God forbid—cajoled into making an ill-informed purchase, it's time to step away from the table and get a second, or even a third, opinion about the product in question.

Patience is the common denominator among successful people in my business. Experience equates to patience with our clients because we have a passion for their welfare, and doing the job right means listening to everything a client says and doesn't say. Sometimes important and touchy subjects relating to family finances remain unsaid in the initial interview. Because I care deeply about the clients I take on, I invest as much time as it takes for them to feel comfortable enough to broach sensitive topics about family finances—a vital part of the financial planning process. Without that kind of patience, I would be unable to serve clients properly. Again, this is the kind of characteristic that separates the seasoned professional from the newcomer.

After doing a lot of listening, we often come to realize that certain people aren't a good match for our services. I know how to recognize an effectively compatible relationship, and I know when to refer someone to another planner—in particular, I do so when I find that after a couple of sessions, I'm just not getting the kind of information I need to be effective. Some potential clients will *never* be comfortable revealing even the basics about their finances or emotional issues in their family—let alone their own goals and expectations.

But most people recognize the need to open up. They know that without enough information, we're like doctors trying to operate wearing a blindfold! Selecting the right financial consultant is a bit like adopting someone into your extended family. For many families, we become a wise aunt or uncle who may step in from time to time to mediate family issues. I often see myself as an objective third party who adds a critical vote when choices must be made about long-term care, Medicaid planning, and other important family issues. Other times, I find myself balancing differing opinions between spouses about how much they need to save and how much they can spend.

So, aside from my gift for mathematics, my ability to provide a financial and economic analysis, and my depth of technical knowledge about annuities and other instruments, many of my clients say they value my patience most. When presenting recommended income plans to them, I take whatever time is necessary for them to thoroughly understand every aspect of the plan and its related products. In my opinion, only then can someone feel comfortable with my recommendations.

When was the last time you bought a car without having a chance to sit inside it, examine the dashboard instruments, and check the latest recommendations from *Consumer Reports*? Add in the tenfold complexity of your financial future and the financial vehicles necessary to drive you comfortably through retirement, and you'll understand why it takes time to do what I do. An experienced professional would *never* push a client to act. Nor will a professional allow herself to be hurried into making hasty recommendations during an initial session. So if a consultant starts dropping product names as you shake hands and sit down for the first meeting, you should wonder whether she has a prepackaged product agenda in mind before she has had a chance to get to know you.

Forming a solid financial strategy can be a very time-consuming process, and it can't be accomplished in a single session. In fact, the process often requires more than two in-depth meetings to get it right. For example, an engineer recently became a client of mine. Engineers are natural builders who understand the importance of properly constructed foundations and supporting structural elements. Not surprisingly, I've met with this engineer on five separate occasions. He has a passion for exploring variables, and he takes great care to make sure he understands every detail—the fine print, so to speak.

I specialize in explaining the fine print. I detail every aspect of every product and product line for my clients, because my work isn't about saving time in the short term. Instead, I'm interested in saving money for the long term, so your money will last you a lifetime. It really doesn't matter to me how many meetings are required to get it right. My prime concern is that my clients will be comfortable with their decisions for a long time to come.

CHAPTER 4

Annuity Specialists:
Separating Reality from Mythology

ONCE, I ATTENDED A WEDDING AND FOUND MYSELF SITTING next to a longtime acquaintance who happened to be a psychologist. She told me about the difference my guaranteed-income strategy had made for the psychological outlook of a mutual client of ours. It made my day. I'd never considered guaranteed-income strategies to be a form of psychological healing before, but why not? We all need peace of mind. Eventually, every one of us will hunger for the sanctuary of a safe, solid retirement without the nagging anxiety over asset preservation. The psychologist helped me realize that too many people fail to see the importance of emotional financial planning. All they think about is the money, but it really isn't about the money—it's about happiness and peace of mind.

You may not be a multimillionaire, but if you invest some of your time to achieve emotional security in retirement, people like me can help you get there. With proper advance planning, it can happen for almost anyone, regardless of their current net worth. For me, the payback of helping others out of a financial quagmire has been more about satisfaction and my own peace of mind than about monetary gain.

I don't mean to sound self-righteous, but I am trying to reach out to everyone entering the financial services industry. I also hope to reach those professionals who might have fallen into the self-denial category. Some of these folks have made a hundred times what I have in the business, but I have earned something even more valuable: the trust of countless people over the past thirty years. In my opinion, that's the best perk you can get in this industry, especially at this particular time in our history.

Not all annuities are alike. Not all financial consultants understand annuities. And not all annuity professionals excel in every area of financial matters, so you need a specialist when you purchase annuities.

Case in point: I recently met with a teacher who was planning to retire and found she had purchased an inappropriate financial product. This discovery was made after a lengthy interview, during which I examined her portfolio and other information.

I didn't probe for the identity of the person who sold her the annuity, nor did I inquire about the salesperson's expertise. I simply told her that the financial product was inappropriate for her situation and explained why. Given her age, retirement goals, and other factors, I suggested she try to recover her funds from the institution. If she did so, she would be able to buy additional retirement income from the State of Connecticut Teachers Retirement Board, where she already had a pension.

As I took a closer look at the teachers' retirement program, I saw that it had some exceptional benefits. The program is an excellent option for teachers because it provides a return on investment no annuity can match, not even the first-rate annuities offered by the consumer-friendly companies I represent. Again, after a careful examination of her assets and retirement goals, I knew she would have been in great shape with the Connecticut plan. The state of Connecticut runs the program quite well, and although I stood to gain nothing from my recommendation, I decided to advocate for her. Other true advocates should be willing to do this sort of thing. I think our numbers are growing, because it's the right thing to do.

I spoke to representatives of the financial institution that held the woman's annuity and convinced them it would be most prudent for both the teacher and the company to return her funds. After a period of negotiation, the situation was resolved, her funds were returned, and she used those funds to increase her retirement benefits through the teachers' retirement program.

Only a select few longtime professional financial consultants and annuity specialists have learned to handle every kind of case, both great and small. We like to tackle large, complex strategies for major estates, but we have also learned to love the smaller individual cases, so we can step in when necessary and help people like the teacher from Connecticut.

You might wonder where I might find time to handle all of this, especially when other, less experienced consultants seem to be in such a rush to conclude meetings and sell you annuities. First, a seasoned professional must be highly disciplined about organizing time, the office, and the business in general. I set out early on in my career to excel in this area, and it carries over to my personal life as well: I am adamant about preserving quality time for my family and friends. They know I care about them very deeply, and this commitment carries back to my clients.

Every morning, I review the details of my day. Every detail of every upcoming meeting is organized in advance, which enables me to remain focused and zero in on essential issues and details. I have cultivated the art of meticulous note taking, and I even tape record the content of my own notes for review before the next meeting with the client. The process of financial analysis also requires extensive research, data gathering, and examination of past, current, and long-term market forecasting.

Behind the scenes, client assets are gauged for long-term survivability in uncertain economic environments. To offset the risks associated with the latter, I review an extensive array of products, paying particular attention to their features, some of which may or may not fit the client's situation. My experience really comes into play when it comes to the fine print on these products. Seasoned pros already have an arsenal of knowledge about the great majority of products. I know the history of those products, how they have changed, where they excel—and where they fail. From there, I review any near-term alterations in product features and balance returns against the existing performance trends in other parts of a client portfolio.

As you can see, what actually goes into a planning analysis in my office is more sophisticated than what you may see and hear when

I make my recommendations. But after I present the net effect of wealth planning to my clients, they always appreciate the effects of the years of industry know-how behind the research and planning process.

I have high expectations for myself and those who work in my office. I set an equally high bar of expectation for anyone I may refer you to, which works both ways: as experience allows me to work with other highly respected financial professionals, they hold me to the same high standard of professional knowledge and conduct that I expect from them. Work with one of them, and you have access to me. Work with someone out of our professional loop, and you may learn the hard way—and meet a hurdle or two in the process.

Financial professionals should respect your time, and they should deliver documents and research materials to you on time. They know how critical time can be in the complex decision-making process. Timely delivery of information is vital, and your questions must be answered as quickly as they come to you, with detail and clarity.

These and other qualities separate true professionals from less-experienced people in the field, but how do you know when you are dealing with the latter? For one, you probably already know the initial warning signs. Perhaps your telephone inquiries are not answered in a timely manner. Your planner may not return your calls at all, and some of your important questions may seem to be conveniently forgotten at subsequent meetings. Perhaps the planner is disorganized, cannot find the answer, or hopes you will forget about the question altogether.

This all highlights the ultimate symptom of incompetence: lack of follow-through. Because these planners are more serious about making money for themselves, and less serious about what they can do for you, they're always chasing a more lucrative deal. As they fervently pursue other priorities, they will ultimately fail to act on much of what they say they will do for you.

But let me say something in the defense of this type of planner: this business requires meticulous research and processing, so it's not for everyone. Many people fail to consider the required years of focus, discipline, organization, education, knowledge, continuing education, and dedication to ethics and advocacy, in addition to the endless hours of meticulous research and processing.

I wish half the advocates I teach could understand a basic truth—the very nature of the annuity itself equates to patience and time. Annuities will not make you rich, but they will keep you secure when other assets bring panic and market debacle. The annuity will provide vital income, but because it is an insurance policy for your money, annuities cannot—and will never—deliver the kind of fast-food overnight windfalls high-risk investments sometimes provide.

Media Coverage of Annuities: Fact-Based Fiction

Newcomers to this business also need to know that referrals are based on client trust. Referrals drive my business, and to earn the trust that leads to referrals, one must learn to truly put the client's needs first. After reading this chapter, I hope you will understand why certain annuities and their representatives have received some bad press. Because of the actions of a misguided few, numerous anti-annuity messages have been released in the media. This toxic misinformation has made me wince with pain, because I know the power of good annuities.

For example, two negative media reports about annuities, one of which appeared in *Consumer Reports* (August, 2006) and another that was featured by NBC News the following month (September 1, 2006), left out 90 percent of the story! They forgot to mention what seasoned pros know all too well: many of the culprits in negative annuity stories have no business selling annuities in the first place. The inferior products portrayed in these media reports also had no business being in the greater marketplace of annuities. I say this because I am a consumer advocate. If I get a bit passionate on the subject of reform, it's because I've dedicated my life to spreading the word about the importance of having some kind of annuity in most retirement plans.

The annuity has been a popular retirement tool in this country for more than a century. Some of your own family members have probably enjoyed secure retirements in large part due to the role of annuities in traditional pension plans. Dependable as this traditional planning tool may be, it continues to get negative coverage in the media.

You might want to consider the source. Since many of these stories are initiated by publications with vested interests in promoting
the securities industry, is it plausible that information for these stories is fed to reporters by people in industries that compete against
annuities? Certain prominent publications rely on advertising revenues from Wall Street brokerage firms and other related entities.
The abundance of securities-related advertising in such publications
is hard to miss.

Sales managers in the securities industry in particular are often
behind the negative coverage of annuities. Why? Because annuities
take principal out of play in the stock market and preserve it as guaranteed income. Annuities have also become particularly relevant to
secure retirement planning since unsettling market conditions have
emerged from late 2001 forward. It might seem threatening to interests in the securities industry. I use the term "seem" here, because
annuities need not rule out investments in securities—far from it.
Annuities have a traditional place in retirement planning and become more and more important as we near and enter retirement. So
why have annuities come under fire in recent years?

As I have said throughout this book, some criticisms of certain
types of annuities are valid. Variable annuities have caused problems
in the past. Most people in the insurance industry will admit it; those
who do not are in denial. In fact, I think many media outlets have
been unbiased when reporting about variable annuities, which can
leave consumers vulnerable to reduced returns. Unfortunately, a minority of variable annuity salespeople fail to reveal those vulnerabili-
ties to consumers. The entire annuity industry suffers an unfair hit
as a result, with wildly generalized speculation pointing to potential
problems with fixed and other types of annuities as well.

The rest of us in the insurance industry have avoided variable
annuities in recent years. But if a news report bundles all annuities
together, painting the entire species in a negative light, the resulting
generalized image creates a dangerously inaccurate picture for consumers and drives consumers toward higher risk, just when many of
them should be in the risk-reduction mode!

How can one point to real "problems" in the absence of volatility? There's only one "problem" with quality fixed annuities—they

leave you unable to risk your principal on speculative instruments of risk, such as stocks, bonds, mutual funds, and so on. Perhaps the worst you can say about a fixed annuity is that it tends to offer conservative returns, but such returns must be conservative because fixed annuities help guarantee the principal you invest. At the same time, those conservative returns guarantee income you cannot outlive.

As we grow older and put more distance between ourselves and our earning years, we want more guarantees and less speculation. We also yearn for more simplicity—not because we are simple-minded, but because our leisure lifestyles become more complex. We want to travel, pursue all sorts of hobbies, and maybe launch a second career, small business, or consulting service. We want our money to work for us in the most efficient manner possible, offering a hedge against unknowns in the market.

I wish the media would report more often on that. In the past, countless media reports have focused on missed opportunities for risk-related gain instead of less sexy conservative income guarantees, but in doing so, they missed the boat about preservation, which underscores the real worries of people in retirement today.

We know the government may not be able to support Social Security forever. We watch corporations whittle away hard-earned pensions. We also know taxation will further erode our nest eggs, along with inflation. Government and corporations have been slowly but steadily shifting the burden of financial planning to the individual. Consider the 2008 government bailouts of financial institutions—individuals, and not institutions or other massive private organizations, will eventually fund the fix through taxation.

At one time, corporations had large departments full of professionals focused on managing, planning, and distributing assets in employee retirement plans. Retirees really didn't get involved in the planning process, and their assets were not vulnerable to loss because honest and reliable people in the corporations had the responsibility of ensuring the safety of their pensions' assets. If those people wanted to keep their jobs, they kept a close watch on the investments, annuities, and other instruments carefully selected for the company's pensioners.

In the past, for example, a person might have worked for a big company for his entire life. At the end of his career, he could relax, forget about the stock market, and rest assured that his monthly pension check would always be there. Baby boomers today aren't so lucky. I've met many boomers who feel overwhelmed by all the different choices for retirement planning. They have to worry about financial details their parents had probably never heard of, and most of them only want one thing—security and guaranteed income in retirement.

Today's boomers also know they don't have the same training the pension planners of yore had, which creates additional uncertainty. Right at the moment when they know they need a good financial planner, they're particularly leery about selecting one. Many of them react to all this uncertainty by burying the retirement issue entirely and refusing to dwell on the inevitable moment when their earning years will be over. And that's when "crisis planning" begins. Crisis planning usually begins after retirement has already begun and a spouse suddenly needs long-term care.

For this reason, financial planning seminars about annuities are packed with people asking lots of questions—but this rarely receives any media attention. With so many people in or near retirement, wouldn't it behoove a news programmer to provide coverage about financial seminars? What if financial planning coverage had a tenth of the attention media gives to sports coverage? I doubt that will ever happen. But for the most part, annuities and their salespeople have been represented as dangerous, and rampant incompetence and negligence of service in stocks, bonds, mutual funds, and other financial sectors has been largely ignored.

Age-Appropriate Use of Annuities

Let's address the issue of age-inappropriate application of the annuity head on. Consider the case of an investor in her early forties who needs to assume more risk during her working years. Would a risk-oriented variable annuity be appropriate for her? If so, what percentage of a younger person's portfolio should be devoted to annuities, and when should she plan to liquidate the variable annuity for the more middle-age-appropriate fixed annuity? At the same time, what features should be attached to the variable annuity during her earning years?

Prepare to be amazed. I have only one answer for this investor: "Forget about annuities—for now." I believe the younger investor should remain in stocks and/or bonds, according to the guidance of the best securities-licensed advisor he can find and afford. If he is fortunate enough to have an employer with a solid 401(k) or some other employer-sponsored investment programs, he should stick with it, because such programs typically offer the same tax-deferral benefits of the better annuities. That's my answer for this investor—period. For him, the time for annuities is yet to come. Sound, calculated risk remains the nature of the game for investors in their twenties, thirties, and even well into their forties. But when I say "sound," I mean that it is your responsibility to consult a qualified securities advisor, because an apathetic investor has only himself to blame for lack of knowledge about his own portfolio gains—and losses.

Variable plans have fees for their insurance portions that cover insurance a younger investor generally doesn't need. Nor does a younger investor need the qualities of the annuity during the critically formative years of his retirement plan, unless he wants to keep a relatively small portion of principal in a safe and untouchable place. If the latter applies, the investor must accept the modest earning curve of a sturdy fixed annuity, in my opinion—and also give up a lot of features, such as 100 percent penalty-free withdrawals for nursing-home care. (Take the lowest possible surrender-charge structure instead.) But again, a younger investor would have to demonstrate a clear need for any kind of annuity in the first place—for example, to protect a grandparent's intended inheritance legacy on behalf of a designated grandchild.

The age-appropriate period begins when clients enter their mid-forties with portfolios substantial enough to begin mid-cycle financial planning. This is the time astute investors begin to examine a variety of safe-haven options for portions of their working retirement portfolio, the goal being to protect portions of earnings from negative market cycles.

So, how much should a forty-five-year-old investor put into his first fixed annuity? It all depends on the size of the portfolio and other factors, but in the annuity business we refer to a basic guideline called the "rule of 100." Basically, as you advance toward the age of 100, you should convert more and more of your assets to safe-money vehicles. The older we get, the less risk we should be willing to take.

But that doesn't mean we need a total commitment to annuities, especially at the latter end of one's life. What kind of annuity, if any, would be best suited for a consumer aged ninety or older? Is it ever appropriate to sell annuities to ninety-year-olds with life expectancies of one to five years? Sales of annuities to seniors in the advanced age bracket have been fraught with misrepresentation, abuse, and outright fraud in some cases, leaving both elderly consumers and their financial planners in deep trouble.

If you are eighty-five, ninety, or older and absolutely determined to buy an annuity, I would only recommend one with a fixed income spread over a five- or ten-year period. But personally, I feel that sales of annuities to ninety-year-olds are almost never appropriate. For the most part, if you are ninety, or even beyond the age of eighty, just say, "No."

However, it is possible that an eighty-year-old wishing to pass an inheritance to specifically designated heirs might choose to do so using a restricted death benefit on an annuity. But even this type of sale is more common among large estates, where enough liquidity exists outside the annuity for major expenses—say, for an heir's college education. In this scenario, more and more carriers have been giving annuity owners the option to force specific income streams on their designated beneficiaries, which negates the possibility of an irresponsible heir's runaway spending spree after receiving a lump-sum check from the insurance company. It also might elevate the need for certain elements of a trust.

Folks in their eighties might also consider the MYGA. Again, this instrument offers a certain degree of liquidity with a modest rate of return and a guaranteed rate similar to that of a bank CD. (If the MYGA offers a higher interest rate than a CD, it almost assuredly carries a higher penalty for early withdrawal.) Either way, the MYGA rarely exceeds a five-year period and should be purchased only if a buyer in her eighties or beyond has ample liquid assets.

Most insurance carriers still offer traditional annuities and MYGAs to people in their eighties and nineties, but I would strongly caution anyone on either the buying or selling side of the ledger to look at the big picture. Are the assets to be placed in the investor's MYGA essentially expendable for the entire accumulation period? Is she adequately covered with enough alternative liquidity to address unexpected financial issues, like in-home custodial care?

That brings us back to the essential issue: what age category is best suited for the purchase of annuities? While I've already addressed annuities for certain investors in their mid-forties, in my opinion, the ideal age for the purchase of an annuity is fifty-five, with maturity and distribution available after ten years (at age sixty-five). People wishing to retire earlier than sixty-five might want to start with a modest amount of principal in an annuity at age fifty (or perhaps in their late forties), and continue to make ever-increasing contributions as they age. Annuities based on specific goals and needs also might be appropriate for people in their mid-sixties to mid-seventies if they have appropriate flexibility in their retirement portfolios.

"Emerging retirees," who are aged fifty-five to sixty-five, ultimately must diversify away from total market risk into safe-harbor instruments, including fixed-indexed annuities early on and, later, fixed annuities and other options. Early in the emerging-retiree period, fixed-indexed annuities protect retirement principal from market erosion, but they still allow the annuity owner to have potentially more earning potential than MYGAs or bank CDs.

For those in the sixty-five-to-seventy-five age group, I have very specific recommendations, including the limitation of surrender-charge periods to no more than ten years and a charge to find the least costly surrender charges available. These investors also need to maximize tax-deferred earnings, which can be tricky if you're simultaneously trying to reduce the impact of surrender fees. Additionally, since annuity products vary widely from one carrier to the next, people in this category must have more than enough money set aside for emergencies. They may also want to maintain a certain asset base in growth-related investments, if not for themselves then for the benefit of their heirs.

But if the ultimate goal is guaranteed income and safety of principal, excessive market exposure for this age group is no longer an appropriate option. If they want income guarantees, they should purchase annuities with guaranteed-income riders. Not all annuities have them, nor do non-bonus annuities necessarily offer maximum earnings. Therefore, we're not only talking about a learning curve but a thorough shopping process, so you can see why it might not be prudent to snap up the first annuity offered in a presentation!

Selecting the right annuity depends entirely upon a client's age, which would determine his income tax-deferral strategy. In the standard discussion of annuities, we often forget one of the prime functions of this type of insurance product—the annuity's unique ability to defer tax on compounded earned income. Tax deferral, along with safety of principal, has been the engine behind the power of the annuity for decades, and new and emerging methods of tax-deferred earnings accumulation have become the icing on the cake for many retirees. With the introduction of income riders to the world of annuities, we also have an excellent tool to create and guarantee the income needed for a fulfilling retirement through an income stream you cannot outlive.

To exemplify annuity payout in a living scenario, let's examine the situation of a sixty-year-old who buys an annuity contract for $100,000. For this example, I have chosen a popular product with an attached **lifetime-income rider** and a fixed-period payout without other options attached, giving our sixty-year-old a ten-year, 10 percent premium bonus contract.

Upon the contract's signing, a 10 percent bonus, or $10,000 worth of value, is added to the annuity. The policy's income rider also guarantees 7 percent growth of annual income, which will be added and compounded annually, tax deferred, until the annuity owner decides to receive income—in this case, at the age of seventy. Given the features of this particular product, including the lifetime rider, a lifetime of income will be paid out at a rate of 6 percent, at the age of seventy and beyond.

The actual dollar amount would come to a payment of $1,102 per month, which sounds fine, but here's where a good financial planner can make a difference. The monthly amount of $1,102 would continue to be paid as long as the annuity policyholder lives, even after the original principal and compounded earnings of the account have been depleted. Should the client live beyond age eighty-five and into her nineties, or—like more and more Americans—beyond the age of 100, the insurance company loses the actuarial gamble, and it loses money. The company wins if she dies early. There's an obvious trade-off for both the annuity provider and the annuity client.

If an eighty-year-old buyer with a living survivor, such as a spouse in her mid- to late sixties, considered this annuity with a different payout option attached, it could still make sense. A different payout scenario would allow a surviving spouse to continue to receive payments, which is why it's so important to look at all options before purchasing annuities. More than a few clients have been improperly directed without being warned about the potential consequences of slapdash financial planning.

Although insurance carriers bear the risk of longevity—meaning that you may continue to draw guaranteed income indefinitely—remember that not all annuities offer walk-away cash-out options upon maturity, and payout schedules vary. To find the real nitty-gritty related to payouts and options, look for a section outlining **annuitization options at maturity** in your annuity contract. The annuity contract may be anywhere from 30 to 120 pages long, with **annuitization methods** (basically payout options and schedules) included at any point in the contract text. Anyone being presented with an annuity should be able to ask for annuitization options at maturity and get straight and immediate directions to that specific part of the contract.

If this seems to be a problem for the financial planner you're dealing with, consider obtaining a second opinion, or another annuity representative altogether!

CHAPTER 5

Annuities under Siege:
Fact, Fiction, and the Elusive In-Between

NOBODY WOULD ARGUE THAT ANNUITIES HAVEN'T COME A long way in the past twenty years, but that can be both a good thing and a bad thing. Industry critics and advocates focus on several issues, foremost of which are excessive fees and surrender charges included in many policies. Complaints about alleged low rates of return run a close second, although annuity returns still outdistance many bank products by nearly two to one. So, let's take a comparative look at the so-called big, bad surrender charge and other types of fees for early withdrawal.

Fees and Surrender Charges

Here are a few examples. One company's contract, which includes a 5 percent bonus to help offset surrender charges, features surrender charges beginning at 15 percent the first year and declining to 0 percent after ten years. Another contract has a **premium bonus** of 10 percent, with the bonus being vested (meaning that the account would receive a certain amount of bonus in a given period of time) and with the surrender charges starting at 10 percent and declining to 0 percent after 10 years. In some states, contracts may have a 5 percent bonus with a surrender charge that starts at 10 percent and declines by 1 percent each year for ten years until it reaches 0 percent in the final year. I personally prefer the features of a contract with a 5 percent premium bonus combined with a modest surrender schedule.

Let's compare these annuity surrender charges with mutual-fund penalties for early withdrawal. First, mutual funds' early withdrawal penalties depend on the class of mutual fund. B-class mutual funds have back-end surrender charges for, just as an example, five-year mutual funds. Such charges typically begin around 5 to 6 percent and decrease at the rate of 1 percent per year. Yet mutual funds also tend to carry a far greater degree of risk, as opposed to the slow-growth aspect (with principal guaranteed) of annuities.

For a close-up on mutual-fund fees, consider the following example of a $10,000 B-class mutual fund. It might incur a $600 penalty for early withdrawal the first year (which is a 6 percent first-year penalty). If market gains were flat that year—showing no gain or loss—the remaining principal would be $9,400. If there was an early withdrawal during the second year (5 percent), given a second year of flat market gain, the penalty would be $500, leaving a remaining principal of $9,500. But this representation of the gross amount of principal doesn't account for the wide range of administrative fees, service charges, and other hidden costs related to the liquidation of a typical mutual-fund account. It's up to the consumer to make sure all such fees are fully disclosed, which may or may not be an easy task, again underscoring the axiom: liquidity is liquidity. Bank CD withdrawal and surrender charges are usually quite modest and certainly have a short-term value, especially for people who are waiting to make more significant financial decisions.

For comparative purposes, I chose a sampling of CD numbers from the latter part of the 2000–2010 decade, a time period marked by troubling recessionary trends and rising inflation. Based on rates garnered from various web sites in that era, as of June 27, 2008, a five-year CD from one of America's largest banking institutions, based on a $10,000 deposit earning 3.88 percent annual percentage yield (APY), charged a 1 percent annual interest penalty for early withdrawal—only $388, which is basically the value of the accrued interest! This account would lose only $403 of a total accumulation of $791 accumulated over a two-year period.

A similar $10,000 five-year CD at a competing consumer bank was earning 3.92 percent annually and charging only 180 days' worth of annual interest as an early withdrawal penalty. A third institution offered a $10,000 five-year CD earning 4.65 percent per year and had an attached 180-day interest penalty for early withdrawal. A fourth bank's $10,000 one-year CD earned 2.17 percent APY and carried a similar 180-day interest penalty for early withdrawal. How liberal can you get?

If you want short-term liquidity in order to remain poised for immediate opportunities, by all means keep some money in bank CDs. I have always suggested maintaining some kind of emergency-cash supplement in money-market funds and CDs; in fact, this is one of the best ways to keep from dipping into your more strategic holdings in annuities and other financial instruments.

But for younger investors, it is equally important to consider the loss of investment potential that comes along with CDs and simple bank savings accounts versus maintaining longer-term positions in well-researched mutual funds. For those who are nearing retirement, hiding cash in bank CDs will cost you—even in the short run—without the tax-deferred earnings, premium bonuses, lifetime-income options, index participation, and other features of quality annuities. People in this category would of course be best positioned if they had increasing assets in annuities in order to mitigate risk. And why not include lifetime-income options, wherein an insurance company assumes your risk and continues to pay you a solid, dependable income, even if you live beyond the allotted ten-year distribution period following the initial accumulation cycle of the annuity!

In short, everything has a place in current and future markets. If your goal is to safely temporarily take a liquidity position and remain outside the prevailing perils of stock market activity—as many investors chose to do in 2008—by all means, consider bank CDs and the like. Upon your reentry into the securities market, of course, you would assume the risk of your principal and potential gains and losses. That's why more and more investors—even younger ones—are pumping increasing amounts of safe-haven savings into conservative instruments that guarantee a stream of income for life.

Annuities protect original principal from risk and offer less risk of flat gain than mutual funds and other instruments. They typically offer features that boost rates of return over bank CDs. A more important factor is the annuity's power of tax deferral, which, combined with premium-bonus and lifetime-income options, can provide a sizable advantage over other retirement planning options.

Meanwhile, mutual funds still offer greater upside market potential, and mutual-fund dividends are reinvested and have lower surrender charges than annuities. So the benefits of both tools bear consideration, with the right annuities gradually replacing certain instruments that carry higher risk in favor of risk-free lifetime income in later years.

Once it's all said and done, the trade-offs abound. So why not come out with it in a sales presentation? In my opinion, surrender charges are not the major issue. The biggest issues are the most incredible: certain salespeople are greedy, unethical, devious, and downright dishonest. Have you heard those terms applied to people in other industries? Certainly, you have. Yet in the annuity industry, these regrettable human traits create monumental consequences when inappropriate company-leveraged products affect vulnerable customers.

It is no secret that high-pressure sales tactics run rampant throughout business. Annuities are no different. Greedy annuity salespeople know how to play against clients' emotions, fears, and the rest. Inappropriate annuities are sometimes sold to the very elderly as a result. In some cases, extremely elderly people have been persuaded to commit large sums of principal without much hope of living to see any real benefit from the annuity. We occasionally hear about such situations (along with other criticisms) and, unfortunately, all too often the critics are right. Ironically, the arguments levied today against annuities echo the old complaints about cash-value life insurance.

Meanwhile, better annuity products do exist, and they're growing in number. They have lower fees, are more consumer-leveraged, and provide better rates of return. But greedy and poorly trained salespeople continue to gravitate toward the high-commission sale which, more often than not, comes from selling a less-than-consumer-friendly annuity.

I've run into some of these people myself. We know who they are, but unfortunately, the industry lacks the power through self-regulation to levy real sanctions for unethical conduct. We need sanctions with teeth. But unlike the more accurate industry criticisms aimed at cash-value life policies and similar products, much of the criticism is little more than hearsay. I'm not blaming the media exclusively. Blogs and forwarded e-mails are an easy and efficient way to scatter disinformation around the globe overnight.

And then there are the "anonymous sources," most of whom come from competing industries, who drop cleverly spun half-truths to reporters hungry to write an exposé. When you know a little about something and get that information out of context, it's easy to come up with wrong information. In many areas of the annuity industry, the damage has already been done. Biased, misleading information can tarnish even the best and most time-seasoned product—even the steadfast high-quality annuity, which certain critics seem to forget.

While less-biased annuity critics are careful to note the appropriate nature of annuities for all sorts of people, the National Association for Fixed Annuities (find it on the Web at www.nafa.us, or contact by phone at 609-720-0882) recently conducted a lengthy survey of media coverage of annuities. The survey concluded that the vast majority of popular consumer financial planning articles contained inaccurate and damaging assessments of annuities.

A disturbing lack of fact-based media perspective continues to misrepresent the annuity's valuable role in retirement planning for one basic reason: once a negative inaccuracy finds its way into print—especially in a so-called reputable publication—it becomes source material for the stories of other publications. The fodder grows and putrefies.

I know you know that. We all know it, but what do we do about it? First, the people who need annuities most should be identified, and these people must be informed about quality annuity products and the companies that provide them. For the purposes of comparison shopping, such consumers also need to know precisely what to look for in a quality annuity. Obviously, not every consultant would be willing to provide such information, and while the media is quick to report on "bad" annuities, they're not all that interested in advocating for "good" ones. Just as annuities served our parents and grandparents very well in retirement, annuities still remain appropriate for many people—modern, innovative annuities in particular.

Annuities deliver one invaluable product: certainty. People like an element of risk, but most crave a strong and consistent element of certainty in their lives as well. As for risk, we take plenty of financial risks before we near our retirement years and probably need to accept some well-advised risk in a diversified portfolio.

Risk may include investments in stock and real estate. But too many people believe they are "investing" when, in truth, they are really just "speculating." To speculate is to make a judgment about something we know a bit about, but for which we lack enough data to make a truly informed decision. Too many financial advisors suffer from the same lack of information and/or analytical skill. So a disturbing number of them simply speculate, based on the advice of someone else they know or from financial newsletters (where editorial credibility may be questionable at best). Many consumers also turn to the advice of charismatic media personalities.

Question: How many financial planners and brokers actually gather information from a range of bona fide sources, crunch the numbers based on a variety of solid historic models, and compare their own results with those of the best minds available?

Answer: Very few, and the brokers and financial planners who do not are among those responsible for these erroneous media stories. By using this sort of consultant, clients may unwittingly speculate for years and become trained to accept the occasionally catastrophic "adjustment" in a portfolio as a necessary part of the retirement savings process. Such clients were once comfortable with an occasional drop in portfolio value, as long as they had enough years to recoup their losses. I think this comfort level changed radically in light of the events of the financial crisis of 2008.

But what many a planner fails to understand is age. Once people begin to actively plan their retirements, they change—dramatically.

The cavalier adventurer of the past is gone. People begin to hold their advisors accountable for every dime squandered on ill-advised investments. They also begin to ask hard questions, even though they may grudgingly hold on to certain stock and bond portfolios.

As they near retirement, people basically begin to feel much less comfortable with risk, and that's when the speculative planner suddenly becomes a thing of the past. I hear it every day when they come to scc me. They come to me because I offer security, and people want security when they near retirement. They need certainty in their retirement incomes.

The last thing they need is the ever-present, nagging fear we experience when we speculate in risk, so the ultimate need for people just entering or nearing retirement is to have a guaranteed income that will never waver, never drop, and never vanish due to changes in the market. In this case, annuities are quite appropriate.

Many people have misconceptions about the use of an annuity. So when new clients come to me, we go through the process of evaluating their income needs, their existing income and assets, and their risk tolerance. Risk tolerance is usually the easy part. When people come to me, risk is the known variable they want to shed. The task is to reduce the tension of any existing risk through the establishment of a guaranteed stream of income.

Clients also tend to know at this point in their lives what risk means to their asset and income base. Many have already experienced the effects a normal 10 percent market correction has on the stock/bond portion of their retirement funds. Many more have experienced catastrophic corrections on Wall Street, and I can see the fear in their eyes when they discuss the subject. Many of the same also express a willingness to accept a lower rate of return in exchange for security, in the form of guaranteed income for life. When they do, I tell them that they have just defined the annuity. Then we move on to the other portions of their financial lives, where an ambitious need for profit and related fears often come to the surface. This is often a difficult and touchy subject.

The vast majority of people want to make enough money to retire comfortably. Driven by fear of failure, they seek safety in risk-related investments. Yet the very investments salving the fear create other fears related to a catastrophic loss of principal. On the part of both the client and the financial professional, it takes patience and careful, methodical discussion to begin the planning process. I've seen clients walk through the door filled with risk-taking bravado, only to discover later—after a lengthy examination of their portfolio—the more conservative people who lie within. Maybe one spouse quietly harbors a more conservative need for guaranteed income, while the other spouse has forged ahead with greater risk tolerance. For such a polarized couple, an annuity might provide some common ground for security, allowing one to speculate in risk while providing security for the other spouse. At some point, advisors have to discover and establish their clients' ideal thresholds of risk-related apprehension. It can be a challenge to uncover the emotions surrounding these two key issues, and this is where experience and professionalism become important.

The next chapter outlines real-life scenarios from my own client files, clearly showing where the rubber meets the road in the successful implementation of your retirement plan.

CHAPTER 6

Annuities at Work:
Life Histories Illustrate the Power of
Peace of Mind

A WOMAN IN HER EIGHTIES CAME TO SEE ME WITH AN OLD BANK CD and two dated fixed annuities. Her goal was to give a block of money to her daughter, while reducing taxes on the interest of the CD. The woman had plenty of money for herself; her income needs were not an issue. Her need was to pass money on to her heir, her daughter, and the purchase of life insurance was out of the question. At her age, the cost of a life-insurance policy would have been an astronomically expensive way to pass money on to her heir, but there was more to the story—which almost always seems to be the case.

The mother wanted to maintain control of the money. Her daughter was something of a spendthrift, and certainly she would be if she were given a lump-sum windfall. Therefore, the mother wanted to have the money paid out over a five-year period from a single source, meaning the money would come from a single source rather than multiple sources requiring additional management (and related fees).

I had an immediate solution for her: a fixed-indexed annuity. This particular annuity came with an attached rider that added enough proceeds to help pay the taxes the daughter would owe upon receiving the annuity money after her mother's death. The annuity would most likely provide more gains than a CD, and the mother would not have to continue tax payments on earnings, as she had with her CD. Upon her mother's death, the daughter would receive the money over a five-year period. During that time, the money would also grow tax deferred, of course, giving it greater income-accumulating power, and the money would safely go to the mother's heir, as she intended, while giving the mother control of the money during her own lifetime.

This situation is a perfect example of how an annuity can be entirely appropriate for an older person. In this situation, the stock market is not a prudent alternative—and that option certainly doesn't carry any guarantees. Nor would a bank CD perform in the same positive way for both the mother and her daughter.

How Do Fixed Annuities Work?

Here's a basic example of how fixed annuities work: If a customer makes a $100,000 principal contribution to an annuity over the cycle of a five-year annuity, the following scenario shows an actual rate of return, year by year, based on recent numbers, as related to a five-year fixed annuity earning 5 percent per annum.

The MYGA fixed annuity earning 5 percent begins Year One with $100,000 and adds 5 percent by the end of the year. Thus, Year Two begins with $105,000, and at the end of that year, 5 percent of $105,000 is added to the total. Accordingly, Year Three begins with $110,250, and at the end of that year, 5 percent of $110,250 is added to the total. Year Four then begins with the resulting $115,762, and at the end of that year, 5 percent of $115,762 is added to the total. At last, Year Five begins with $121,550, and at the end of that year, 5 percent of $121,550 is added to the total—resulting in a grand total of $127,628.

At the end of Year Five, the customer can walk away with $127,628—not bad for five years without risk. With this particular product, the client can ask for a check from the insurance carrier for $127,628, or the client can move, or "roll," the cash in her account into another tax-deferred vehicle, thereby avoiding taxation for the moment, to allow the continuation of tax-deferred compounding interest. If she opts to cash out and take a lump-sum payment, she gets a check for $127,628 and pays the required taxes.

With fixed-indexed annuities, you have a choice of options that would determine the crediting method of your annuity. Given that the point-to-point method is generally the most readily understood, let's start there. Additional factors may be combined, including **caps**, which are earnings limitations and chosen rates of participation in further market earnings made by the annuity provider.

Before we get started, note that the point-to-point method works particularly well in gradually growing economic conditions. A longer-term contract works best to absorb periodic economic downturns. The irony is that a long-term annuity strategy may sound as if it relates to the standard **long-term asset-allocation strategy** seen in various forms of risk-related financial planning. The difference lies in the true nature of risk. Safe-retirement strategies use instruments that guarantee principal, placing only the earning potential of the principal in question when using fixed-indexed annuities; other annuities offer more secure guarantees of earnings at lower rates than fixed-indexed annuities. In contrast, standard financial planning involves mutual funds and other securities that offer greater profit potential but place principal entirely at risk.

Using annual point-to-point crediting. The **point-to-point crediting method** is a method of calculating annual annuity-account earnings starting at the starting point of a given year and concluding at the ending point of the same year. It is calculated by subtracting the starting number of the market index at the time of contract purchase from the index number exactly one year later, and then dividing the result with the beginning number. For example: If the Dow was 9,500 at year's end and 8,500 when the contract was signed, the result is 1,000. From there, divide 1,000 by the Dow's beginning number (8,500), which equals 0.12, or 12 percent. This final number, 12 percent, can be modified by caps, spreads, participation rates, and so on before being added to the annuity owner's account each year.

In this model, our hypothetical annuity has an earnings cap, or participation rate, set at 9.75 percent. Thus, a 9.75 percent earnings increase is credited to the account. Additionally, with many annuities the carrier also risks the unlimited potential payout of a lifetime of income for the annuity owner, should the owner live beyond the maturity/payout period of the original annuity contract.

Test any one method during various markets over a period of time and you will see it outperform the others. Actuarial tables show that such methods equal out over a thirty- to forty-year period, but which one bears the test of shorter, ten- to fifteen-year periods? Like conventional planning, which may incorporate a mix of securities in a given retirement portfolio, it might be best to employ several different crediting methods to capture growth opportunities during various economic conditions.

Again, we're talking about regulating earnings in the safe, but more limited, environment of annuities. If you really want to go after risk-related market returns, get the best qualified advice for entering the securities market rather than expecting stock-market returns from fixed-indexed annuities. Fixed-indexed annuities are what they are: safe-haven vehicles for accumulating some earnings in favorable market conditions and locking in those gains while preserving principal. As people advance into their retirement years, some may prefer to maintain some level of risk in the market. But even for those clients, I always recommend placing a good foothold on the solid ground of lifetime income and principal guaranteed.

Although I'm the first to admit that annuities are not appropriate for everyone, if you need an element of certainty in your income planning, certain types of annuities may be right for you. Prominent publications like the *Wall Street Journal* (May 12, 2002) and *Smart Money* (November 1997) have for years reported favorably about certain income annuities (which are also called immediate annuities), describing them as something everyone should at least consider. As stated earlier, immediate or income annuities, which are also called single premium income annuities (SPIAs), can provide a lifetime of income, either over a specific time period or a combination selected by the policyholder. Either way, immediate/income/SPIA annuities allow income payments to begin almost immediately—within thirty days to a year.

An intermingling of income annuities, fixed annuities, and fixed-indexed annuities are part of what I call my **Safe-Retirement Incomer** mix. The income annuity gives you immediate income, letting the balance of your funds grow tax deferred until you need income from those (tax deferred) funds. Also, the growth mechanisms in different annuities will vary. The fixed-indexed annuity will always guarantee your principal while allowing the balance of your retirement funds to grow more quickly. However, the fixed-indexed annuity does not allow you to use the money as readily. And while the insurance company guarantees income for a period of time through the income annuity, the fixed-indexed annuity needs more time to do what it is supposed to do.

The fixed-indexed annuity has the potential to earn a higher return while at the same time protecting principal; some fixed annuity products offer 4 to 5 percent returns for income purposes while having the potential to earn a high rate of return according to a market index (the S&P, Dow, NASDAQ 100, or the FTSE, for example). Some carriers use more than just U.S. market indices as units of measure: many offer options on foreign markets, like EuroStoxx50 and Hong Kong's Hang Seng Index, or even on commodities like gold.

I like the flexible nature of the Safe-Retirement Incomer because the mix of income and fixed-indexed annuities satisfy a number of emotional needs at once. The income annuity gives guaranteed cash flow for budgeting everyday needs. The fixed-indexed annuity satisfies an earnings ambition without triggering the fear factor of risk-related investments. The fixed-indexed annuity eliminates fear because it guarantees principal and a certain level of return—yet the client stands to gain more return if the market grows.

As for the near future and the present, the annuity industry seems to be moving toward greater client flexibility, probably because of increased demand among clients, industry critics, and safe-retirement advocates like me. While flexibility means a greater degree of control and choices for clients, new products are emerging to provide a stream of income the client cannot outlive. They also offer an ongoing array of control mechanisms, including cashing out of the annuity at a given point in time and walking away without penalty.

Consumers should also look for new products, including all of the aforementioned, with the ability to continue earning interest on unpaid money while receiving monthly income payments during the distribution cycle of the annuity. I call those and other combinations "hybrid" products with an endless mix of consumer-friendly options. Because products like these are emerging with greater regularity, I think it has become more essential than ever for annuity representatives to be licensed to sell securities. If they are, they're continuously educated to better understand the global economy.

One recent innovation is a ten-year annuity with five-year point-to-point options and no bonus. In this scenario, the client receives no earnings credits to his account until the annuity's five- and ten-year anniversaries. Yikes. After hearing about other types of annuities, how would this have any advantage whatsoever? Well, this hybrid product is a stripped-down streamlined earner because it allows the annuity holder to gain 100 percent of the advantage of upside market activity. Forget about earnings caps, spreads, and participation rates of other fixed-indexed annuities—this one gives the annuity owner full market participation along with the insurance carrier, but without risking principal or previous market earnings. It's possible because the client no longer requires the usual annual "lock" on minimum earnings, which allows the insurance carrier to buy into longer-term options in market indices. Yes, you assume a form of risk by forfeiting a minimum of annual gain, but you also remain fully vested to earn indexed credits.

Another emerging product to look for is an annuity with long-term care (LTC) benefits attached. For many years, I have advised consumers to exercise caution when considering the purchase of cost-prohibitive LTC insurance, since LTC benefits can be found in, or added to, other, more comprehensive insurance products. Unless you purchase LTC insurance at a very young age, it becomes virtually unaffordable for those who really need it. And for young people able to afford it, LTC premiums take valuable funds out of play at a time when their money should be in securities and other investment markets. That includes real estate, in the form of an aggressive pay-down strategy aimed at debt-free home ownership!

Just make sure when considering LTC insurance that your overall asset mix justifies LTC coverage. It may be more effective to cover these unexpected costs through careful planning with other assets. For example, with some of the LTC annuities now available, a client can walk away from the contract after ten years, more or less, if she never needed to use her LTC benefits.

Last but not least, as consumers are becoming more and more aware of punishing surrender charges, industry trends will move toward dwindling surrender periods—less than 10 years at the very least, with surrender charges beginning at less than 10 percent during the first year and declining more precipitously each year thereafter.

All of these are necessary improvements, and most are already available. New forms of hybrid annuity packaging will continue to evolve over time, which means that consumers can expect and therefore demand shorter surrender periods and reduced surrender charges along with lifetime income options, increasing amounts of payouts for survivors and beneficiaries, and annual earnings with LTC riders for medical emergencies.

How Do the Carriers Do It?

Annuities benefit both the insurance carrier and the customer—otherwise, why would the insurance company sell them? When the insurance carrier goes to the market with $100,000 of a client's funds to purchase options for the client's crediting methods, here's what tends to happen.

Perhaps the carrier contacts an option broker to buy one-year options with 100 percent participation of all index upsides, with no caps on upside potential, tied to the S&P 500. The carrier may contact an option broker to buy options in an index. In this example, the carrier has only $3,500 to spend on options in an index, because the balance of the $100,000 principal is needed to purchase a variety of bonds, as with any other fixed annuity. Therefore, parameters will be put on the option to make them affordable. The carrier does so by creating a **spread**, a cap, or a participation rate. For example, if the spread is 1 percent and the S&P is up 4 percent, the customer's annuity contract will be credited with the remaining 3 percent.

You may be wondering about those caps I mentioned earlier. A cap is a limitation placed on increased credits. If a market index is up 6 percent and the policy places a 4 percent cap on a customer's earnings, the customer's account would receive a 4 percent credit.

The **participation rate** is somewhat different, allowing the policyholder to receive a certain percentage of upward movement of an index (for example, the S&P). Thus, a participation rate of 70 percent on a 7 percent market gain would mean the client would be credited with 4.9 percent earnings that are locked in (as would any earnings in a fixed-indexed annuity).

Options become more affordable for the insurance company through the placement of participation rates, spreads, or caps in annuity policies. The insurance company might pass lower costs on to the client through a one-year option without a spread, but with a 6 percent cap and a 100 percent participation rate.

Inappropriate Annuities

Now let's get to the nitty-gritty of the inappropriate use of annuities. The first case involves a chemist who retired from XYZ Company, a major drug company based in Connecticut. The chemist had a comfortable pension and a seven-figure 401(k), but he received very little retirement guidance from his company. His employer's credit union, which was located on XYZ Company's property, did have an insurance salesperson, but the company, the credit union, and the salesperson failed to inform the chemist that the salesperson was not an employee of the credit union *or* XYZ Company.

Given the credibility of being surrounded by XYZ Company and its employees, the chemist naturally assumed the insurance salesperson was endorsed by XYZ Company, but that's not always the case, both in banks and in credit unions. This particular insurance salesperson had automatic credibility and trust with XYZ Company employees without the knowledge and experience to back it up. This sort of thing happens every day, nationwide, in banks, credit unions, and everywhere else.

The chemist spoke with the insurance agent about converting his 401(k) money into supplemental income to add to his pension. Without doing any planning, the agent later called him at home with a recommendation. The chemist was a bit distracted at the time and open to persuasion. The agent was persuasive indeed, subconsciously drawing on the chemist's trust and suggesting a real association with XYZ Company. The following day, one of his last days with XYZ Company, the chemist signed an annuity contract, turning over a large portion of his 401(k) money to the agent and the annuity provider.

Weeks later, he began to have a creeping sense of apprehension over having signed the annuity contract without further examination. At the same time, regretting what he had done, he felt locked into the annuity because his right to review the annuity contract had expired—along with his right to cancel it. Eventually, he was able to get his money back, but only after he realized that without a full plan and a full understanding of his needs, he would not be able to make an educated decision about his financial future.

So why was this annuity so inappropriate? One, his pension already provided a lifetime of guaranteed income, an outcome he could not outlive. He had no reason to be fearful about his retirement income, and the manner in which the annuity was sold to him was reprehensible, to say the least. No real advance interview or asset evaluation had been performed. Nothing had been done to determine the appropriate application of any annuity—let alone the inappropriate nature of the annuity he was so quickly sold. He never received a decent, comprehensive explanation of the nature of the product itself, and he'd never had the opportunity to ask enough questions to feel comfortable about the product.

Information You Should Know

More than a few of us have experienced the intimidation of the kind of high-pressure sales tactics that left the chemist feeling victimized and thoroughly disrespected. Unfortunately, this happens too often in the financial planning industry because people lack the time, patience, and energy to educate themselves about investment alternatives, leaving them vulnerable to unethical sales practices. For the sake of convenience, some people place their trust in someone they hardly know. It's equally unfortunate that many who claim to be financial services professionals are anything but professional, and they're often unwilling or unable to supply critical information.

For example, one vital bit of information people might need to know is the annuity's payout methods. What should one expect? You might not always get a clear answer, like the chemist: he probably would have remained with his 401(k) payouts had he been given the whole picture. So before you consider annuities or invite a representative to give a presentation, consider the following before making the appropriate decision:

Payout schedules vary, which gives a prospective annuity buyer many options. In the industry, we have historically called the payout phase **annuitization**. Historically, after an annuity owner left the accumulation phase of the annuity and began receiving a routine schedule of payments—**distributions**—from the annuity, she would be considered to be in the annuitization phase. Today, however, more options are available. The following have been in place for several years and provide a good concept of payout, or **annuitization-distribution**, procedures. They come in several basic categories, including the following.

The fixed-period method. With a **fixed-period method** annuity, holders receive equal monthly payments during a fixed period of time, typically from five to thirty years. The determined length of the payout period is generally up to the annuity owner, although the time periods offered by various annuity carriers may differ. If payout periods are of interest to you when shopping for annuities, remember that the end result is always the same—payments will continue until the end of the fixed period determined by the annuity owner and then cease altogether.

The life-annuity method. With the **life-annuity method**, life-annuity owner, known as the payee, chooses to receive a dependable sum of money each month for his lifetime. Upon the death of the payee, all payments stop, and the annuity provider is not obligated to make further payments to heirs. That might sound like a good thing for the insurance company offering the annuity, and it is if the payee dies during the period of time the company expects him to pass away. It can be much more costly for the company, however, if the annuity holder lives longer than statistical tables predict—and that becomes a financial lifesaver for the annuity holder. As life expectancies grow with every new medical and nutritional breakthrough in this country, the life-annuity option has become more popular. Beneficiaries who wish to leave a legacy to their heirs must be sure to include guaranteed payments in their annuity option.

Emerging payout options. A variety of new payout trends called **emerging payout options** are enhancing the flexibility of annuities, both in the way they grow and continue to grow as proceeds are being paid out. Some annuities now offer the option of receiving a lifetime of income without actually annuitizing the annuity contract, which means that you can set an amount of money that would never decrease and would be guaranteed each month for the rest of your life. Even though you are receiving this monthly payment for the rest of your life, the balance of principal in your annuity could remain in play, allowing it to benefit from any growth accumulated by the annuity provider in the form of "index credits."

Generally, you must select this optional contract rider when you buy the annuity in order to take advantage of the specified compounding growth within the income account that would let your annuity grow during both the accumulation and the distribution phase, keeping the unused portions of your annuity at work as long as possible. Some carriers charge a fee for this type of rider. Others offer the option free of charge, but all offer guaranteed income and a guaranteed percentage of ongoing growth in the balance of your annuity account.

Beneficiary protection. Annuities can be used as a tool to pass assets to heirs in a controlled manner, with most carriers offering ways to restrict beneficiaries from receiving a lump-sum distribution from the annuity upon the owner's death. These **beneficiary restriction forms** can be completed at any time in order to have your beneficiary receive lifetime payments as a death benefit, rather than a lump sum—providing the beneficiary with a genuine legacy instead of a single vulnerable check. These annuities should offer restriction forms as well as the highest earnings rates and caps available.

College plans. If a representative suggests annuities as a college savings plan, be very careful. Annuities essentially offer tax-deferred earnings, but withdrawal may trigger a 10 percent IRS penalty if withdrawals are made before the contract owner turns 59½. Thus, parents and grandparents may want to consider IRS 529 education plans as better college savings strategies.

Even though a planner might outline all sorts of annuity liquidity options offered now and in the future, bear in mind that annuities are still long-term contracts. Annuities should not be purchased by people who might need access to the principal contribution before the contract matures. That's the bottom line for annuities, regardless of any pregame sales rhetoric you may hear.

So What's the Best Bet?

I've had a lot to say about incompetent and unethical annuity salespeople. You could just as easily encounter the same level of incompetence when considering mutual funds, managed accounts, exchange-traded funds (ETFs), and all other investment options. Are ETFs, managed accounts, and mutual funds appropriate for everyone on the planet? Of course not! Will some planner insist that they are, at some hapless investor's expense? Of course he will! Would it pay everyone with a retirement portfolio to park all of their life savings with a financial manager who charged a 1.5 percent fee? No! On top of all of that, I can't think of a single manager in the world who could put the brakes on a market crash.

Let's take the word "annuity" out of this discussion for a moment and substitute real-estate insurance trusts, bonds, Dow blue chips, or any stock on the S&P. Nothing in the financial world is a sure thing if it's improperly applied to someone's portfolio, which is why experienced financial advisors, brokers, planners, and insurance professionals have become so important. Unfortunately, the best professionals are few and far between, with learn-by-earn wannabes filling the void. Meanwhile, too many consumers take the hit because they sometimes fail to question a referral from friends or family members. Miracles worked by Uncle John's "financial wizard" may be totally wrong for cousin Anne.

I wish I could give you a certain cure-all, an absolutely surefire financial template. Truth be told, financial forecasting will always remain an inexact science at best, and more speculative art than science at worst. Of that, you may be certain, given the emotional nature of trading and a host of other factors.

Returning to our model of well-balanced greed and fear, just how much risk should you expect in a balanced account? A man walked into my office with balanced accounts in various mutual funds. He'd had them for years, but when I asked him about his ten-year average annual return, he could only give me a puzzled look. He had no idea. So I asked him, "If I could give you a guaranteed 3 percent return over a ten-year period, and you averaged 2.3 percent with a mutual fund, would this be acceptable to you?"

"Maybe," he replied, "given the losses of the last decade." For someone else, however, a 3 percent return would be entirely unacceptable, which points up something every investor must know— not every investor views risk tolerance in the same light, and the same goes for financial professionals. Not every advisor favors a balanced portfolio, nor do they unanimously favor a low to medium level of risk tolerance, nor will they tell you where they lean in terms of risk. Not necessarily.

To counterbalance the risk variable among financial planners, look for a professional who puts her client first. You will begin to recognize this individual by an ability to really listen. This listening process involves more than just a simple chat or two—it requires an applied methodology. Such methodology is necessary to determine your true risk tolerance.

Then we take it a step further. To act as a bona fide fiduciaries, planners must put their needs in the back seat. If clients clearly lean toward an extreme tolerance for risk, some planners jump at the chance to immediately sell a client a high-risk instrument. But planners have a fiduciary duty to give clients the most prudent course of action—even for high-risk investors. This may include recommendations for income guarantees to balance risk, and such recommendations come from experience-based judgment.

As an advocate, I have had to intervene when others have applied inappropriate financial products to clients' portfolios. Remember the example of the teacher in Connecticut who had been sold inappropriate products? I had to step in and request a refund from the company. To get that refund, I had to maintain pressure when the first company resisted, but I know the inner workings of the business, so the teacher and I prevailed in the end.

Your financial professional should be willing to go to bat for you in this type of situation. Although I had nothing to gain, it gave me great satisfaction to solve the teacher's problem and suggest that she turn the principal into additional retirement income with the state teacher pension program. I make no money from that kind of advice, but a good advocate does it because it is the right thing to do.

Likewise, helping the XYZ Company chemist resulted in no commission for me. I enjoy pro bono work, knowing that spreading a bit of goodwill might come back to me in a positive way. Financial professionals in the business for the long haul know pro bono work can be a wise investment in building a solid practice, and those who are in it for the fast buck fail to understand this basic principle of building long-term relationships, trust, and referrals. They make sales according to their own needs, not yours.

Through all the years I've been in this business, I've seen it all. Like many experienced financial professionals, my scope of knowledge goes well beyond annuities as it must in order for me to offer clients a balanced perspective. Diverse financial knowledge is essential to guide clients through a maze of different retirement planning options, so I find myself working beyond annuities from time to time.

For example, I recently developed a relationship with a client who held a lot of savings in a bank. He planned to retire that year and wanted to convert those savings to income. It would have been an easy task if it weren't for his other challenge: protecting his money from taxation. How many times do we consider the purchase of something expensive without considering the additional cost of sales tax? When the final tally is added to the price of a new car, for example, a good bit of the "sticker shock" comes from the unavoidable hundreds or thousands of tax dollars added to the bottom line. Fortunately, in financial planning, we have a few tools to ease the burden of taxation on your income earnings. The client with bank savings was keenly aware of that. He wanted to defer taxation on his earned income, and he knew about the power of compounding returns with annuities—that tax payments can be delayed as annuity earnings grow. He also wanted to see a fair rate of return.

The client and I worked together to develop a plan in which he would receive a fair rate of return, guaranteed income, and tax deferral. I went over every detail of the plan with him, using conservative numbers and a combination of annuity products. To achieve his retirement goals, we repositioned assets into a combination of annuity products, including a fixed-indexed and an immediate annuity.

But he and his wife had other needs as well: she wanted to move up from their $200,000 home to a $450,000 house. Here, I had to walk an emotional tightrope and turn mediator, because the numbers were clear. If they wanted a solid, sustainable retirement plan, they couldn't afford to make such an expensive jump in housing costs. I knew I had some emotional hurdles coming, so I carefully outlined the reality of the numbers over the course of three meetings. I then gave the wife enough time to digest and thoroughly understand the facts, allowing her to see the reality of the situation without forcing my own opinions. After reviewing the facts, she realized the purchase of the house would have prohibited many other things in retirement. In the end, they both agreed that the purchase of another home would cost them dearly, both in terms of peace of mind and the ability to enjoy their retirement.

Another client had been buying financial products from ABC Company for twenty-five years. Not surprisingly, he had quite a bit of money tied up in products suggested by the company. He had been doing business with an "affiliated" ABC Company agent versus a truly independent financial planner. An affiliated agent tends to offer products within a specific company line, even though such products may have limitations, excessive fees, and little flexibility. How can an affiliated planner possibly avoid making inappropriate recommendations? At some point, a client's situation will certainly override the limitations of a single product line. My new client had already arrived at this conclusion, which is why he came to me. Consumers are becoming more savvy about using a traditional (one-company) salesperson versus going with the unbiased advice of a truly independent planner.

The ABC Company agent was not at all pleased, of course, when my client left him a message saying he was making a move to an independent planner. In fact, after my client announced his change to a new retirement strategy, the ABC Company agent refused to ever talk to him again! After a twenty-five-year relationship with my client, the agent refused to respond to his call with a courteous "Good luck."

No wonder the agent lost his client after twenty-five years. If he couldn't find the time to call a former client back and wish him well, how much time did he really spend talking with his client or performing behind-the-scenes planning on his client's behalf? Did he merely take the client's business for granted, shove a few standard— or substandard—products at him, and then move on to new business? People like that see it all as part of the cost of doing business, favoring arm's-length deals over real client relationships and dwelling almost entirely on the development of new business, which inevitably leads to the loss of old business and more than a few unhappy former customers. It really is a strange mentality to me, but it is all too common.

The difference, as my new client put it, is that he trusts people like me far more, even though he's known me less than a year. He says it's because I've spent more time with him in this short period than his former agent spent with him in twenty-five years of doing business. Every client deserves that kind of attention from her financial professional.

Each year, I host an annual client appreciation party, and at one year's party, I overheard a conversation in which one of my clients bragged to another about the method I'd used to buy him a new car. Actually, it wasn't that big a deal—I simply searched his financial records with a fine-toothed comb until I found excess funds that could be extracted without affecting his lifestyle in retirement. We directed that extra money toward the purchase of a new car. Not everything has to be bottom-line conservative in safe-retirement advocacy, after all. When you plan properly for guaranteed income and adjust your lifestyle to that income, extra money sometimes appears as if by magic. It's not magic, of course—just good retirement planning based on income guarantees. The car-buying client had been with me for some time and was comfortable with my financial plan. I'd been able to stay in his comfort zone and still find enough extra cash for the car.

All annuities are not all things to every portfolio. Solid relationships with clients and quality insurance providers are at the heart of building a dependable business. Reputable planners always work hard to build relationships with insurance companies that have demonstrated a commitment to consumer-leveraged products and services. Therefore, it should not be surprising that these companies are some of the most financially secure and resilient in the world, offering products with low fees, better returns, and greater flexibility for the consumer. All you need to know is who they are, and an experienced and ethical annuity consultant will give you that information.

CHAPTER 7

Defining a Financial Professional:
The Latitude of Attitude

RÉSUMÉS. I HAVE A LOVE–HATE RELATIONSHIP WITH THEM BE-cause they say so little about the real person behind the statistics. I have seen people excel in this business without much formal education because they have a high level of intrinsic intelligence, a voracious capacity for learning, and the integrity to build a solid career through appropriate, guaranteed-income–based retirement planning.

Conversely, some in my business have little more than a high school diploma, completion of a rudimentary sales course, and the sole motivation of making money. Armed with a handful of company brochures and photocopies of financial news articles, they look the part but lack the proper training, which today includes passing examinations and licensing requirements.

What Should Your Advisor's Résumé Include?

All states require that people who sell annuities have a life-in-surance license. Insurance agents are additionally regulated by their respective state's department of insurance or insurance commission, which is usually listed in the phone directory under state regulatory agencies. Through such departments, most states now offer online resources to check the credentials, background, and disciplinary history of every licensed annuity and life-insurance agent in the state.

Insurance agents can advise clients about insurance features, the workings and application of fixed annuities, surrender charges, and all things related to insurance products. They are not allowed, however, to discuss securities or any aspect of financial planning involving securities. Some insurance licensees call themselves "financial planners" without having enough knowledge or licensing to broach the subject of securities, which is germane to the topic of financial planning in any real sense. A financial planner who lacks a securities license is often drawn into a discussion involving the value of securities and how they relate to the purchase of annuities. This is particularly worrisome when a conversation turns to variable annuities, which are regulated by the Securities & Exchange Commission (SEC).

As of this writing, while fixed and fixed-indexed annuities and other insurance products still remain under the aegis of insurance regulators, a troubling haze has settled over the regulatory issue. If insurance agents cannot talk about securities in any sense of the term, how can they give advice about fixed-indexed annuities or other securities-related insurance products without compromising the intent of securities law? In order to be safe and properly educated, insurance licensees must look to the future and obtain proper securities registration, beginning with Series 6, Series 63, and Series 65 registrations. The amended Investment Advisors Act of 1940 clearly defines a licensed advisor as "… any person who, for compensation, engages in the business of advising others, either directly or through publications or writings, as to the value of securities or as to the advisability of investing in, purchasing, or selling securities, or who, for compensation and as part of a regular business, *issues or promulgates analysis or reports* [italics mine] concerning securities …"

A properly licensed registered investment adviser (RIA) registers by filing Form ADV with his state's securities department and/or with the SEC. As a rule of thumb, RIAs register with the SEC when they manage more than $25 million in assets. Those with less than $25 million under management register with their state securities division. Either way, they must adhere to other requirements and follow standard practices, including:

- Thoroughly evaluating clients' risk tolerance and needs based on retirement assets.

- Providing related wealth-management guidance—often with the help of other licensed professionals—including tax and trust advice, charitable giving consulting, and estate and financial planning services.
- Routine monitoring of the progress of every client portfolio, including providing routine performance reports and evaluations.

RIAs use securities brokers/dealers and clearing firms to implement trades or sales of any securities instrument. It is also important to note that securities-licensed advisors are not recommended by the SEC—they are merely subject to SEC rules and regulations, which require certain levels of licensing for specific activities.

A Series 6 licensee can, for example, sell variable annuities and mutual funds. That ability alone might give the licensee a more balanced approach to the annuity market. But without at least a Series 65 license, how could anyone call himself a financial planner in the legally sanctioned sense of the word? While a fully licensed securities broker must also have a state-specific insurance license to sell annuities and other insurance products, I think it is immeasurably important to have both types of licensing. The additional knowledge and the accordingly balanced perspective of a securities licensee can make an important difference, especially as clients begin to merge into safe-retirement vehicles and away from securities-oriented strategies.

My Own Résumé

My wife and I live on the Connecticut shoreline of the Atlantic Ocean, one of the most beautiful spots in southern New England. I'm living the American dream, a dream I discuss in many planning sessions. My clients have dreams, but so many believe they will never achieve them. I often become a can-do coach who can reawaken their dreams.

To be able to live beside the ocean every day is the realization of a lifelong dream, and it didn't come easily. I came from modest means, so from a very young age, I always had a job—I worked with children as a camp counselor (which paid a whopping $125 for an entire summer) and had a paper route. My time spent at the summer camp led to my ocean dream, and the dream helped fuel my desire to succeed.

Along the way, I learned the intrinsic value of the dollar. At age sixteen, I managed to land a job at a shoe store in New Britain, Connecticut. This was a very big deal: I held regular hours, punched a time card, and received a regular paycheck, just like the grown-ups around me. Filled with pride, I decided to become the top shoe-polish salesman. In my mind, I wasn't just selling shoe polish. I had become a store specialist who received a $1 commission for selling a can of shoe polish. This was an astounding sum at the time, so I went for it with gusto, eventually moving up to become the top shoe— and shoe polish—salesman in the store.

I learned to love what I did to the point of volunteering to clean the store on Sundays, when we were closed. I was making $35 a week and thought I was rich. I'd discovered two very valuable commodities in business: the ability to specialize and the art of becoming keenly passionate about my work.

I took my $35-a-week riches and bought a motorcycle. The daredevil aspects of bike riding introduced me to a love of flying, which inspired me to join the Civil Air Patrol and eventually apply to the U.S. Air Force Academy. After applying to the Academy, I earned a healthy dose of humility and another important business lesson: dreams are great, but sometimes we need to cheerfully realign our dreams with reality. I was unable to qualify for flight training, so a ten-year postcollegiate commitment to the Air Force suddenly made no sense whatsoever. No jets, no way. It was time for a dream realignment, a process I would one day learn to apply to my business.

I went instead to Central Connecticut State University, picked up an avid interest in mathematics, and maintained my commitment to work at the summer camp through my college years. I went full circle in a way—swapping the *Top Gun* dream for a home by the sea. To that end, I would apply all my practical, achievable resources in business and throughout the community.

I had some of my most memorable life experiences at that camp. I really felt needed there, and I knew the place inside and out. Like my experience at the shoe store, I would donate my preseason weekends to the camp, riding up on my motorcycle to mow the lawns. I felt it had to be done, and I was the only one to do it. I mowed lawns, cleaned the cabins, and made sure a punch list of necessary maintenance tasks was accomplished before the campers arrived.

Why? First, I had fun. But I also helped a lot of kids find themselves at that camp. In a way, they helped me find myself, too, and I knew I was really there for the kids. Lots of college kids began moving in different directions at that age—in that era in particular—but the summer camp kept things in perspective for me. Looking back, I now realize that my values today reflect some of the values I'd begun to form back then, when I learned to really care about people outside my own family. Caring became a vital part of being alive. It led me to become who I am today, and yet I still wonder if I'm doing enough. Should I know more about what I do? Have I considered every possible avenue to help hardworking people realize their own retirement dreams?

Thanks to that experience, when I entered the insurance business I was able to place the needs of my clients ahead of my own from day one. I've told you as much as I can about my own background—not just items on a résumé—to help you identify the person you choose to help protect your life savings in retirement. Please understand that there are lots of us out there who have the same helping spirit, which may not be important in every trade, but in mine, I consider it to be essential.

After college, at the tender age of twenty-four, I founded, owned, and operated a property and casualty insurance business. I've also worked for a variety of insurance companies and always maintained a top-ten position in sales with every one of them, despite the fact that I always adhered to a conservative planning philosophy.

I've been in the insurance business for more than thirty years, at one juncture owning and managing three different businesses at once—the insurance agency, a real-estate agency, and even a motel! In the real-estate business, I loved helping people in little and big ways, such as helping people complete the largest purchase most will ever know, their home. The motel was an ongoing learning process. I wasn't always prepared for the amazing variety of problems humans can create for themselves literally overnight. One of our guests clogged a toilet one evening but failed to tell us about it before morning. When the wife awoke in the wee hours, she stepped directly into a pond of water. (I still can't figure out how the family went to sleep with water seeping under the bathroom door.) I won't go into further illustrations of the unexpected in the motel trade, but I did learn one solid lesson from the experience. You will *never* be able to plan for every unknown, no matter who you are or what you do. This is why appropriate retirement planning is so important. I *can* guarantee retirement income, even if you insist on taking risks in other areas.

I learned valuable lessons from those noninsurance businesses and gained invaluable experience I would never get at any college or university. I saw the tears, for example, when a family was denied a home loan because of poor financial planning. They had too much debt, and the husband decided to buy a new car, out of the blue, while they were looking for a new home. The husband's real-estate agent failed to tell him that a new-car loan would jeopardize his ability to get a mortgage. What a tragedy! It's much easier to buy a new car *after* you buy a new home, but I'm sure the husband threw up his arms and said, "Who knew?" Someone should have told him, but maybe his real-estate agent was too new to the business to know the perils of inappropriate mortgage planning. It *is* all about planning, isn't it? In virtually every corner of the financial realm—stocks, bonds, real estate, or motel management—planning comes first. Without a plan, you may find yourself without a roof over your own head.

Between 1990 and 1998, I sold all of the businesses so I could concentrate on just one thing—retirement planning. I studied for and received my Series 65 licenses to become an RIA and returned to my core skills: math and helping people.

The Importance of Giving Back

Several years ago, I founded the Reindel Heritage Foundation, which makes charitable donations to specific individuals and organizations. As a managing partner of the Reindel Heritage

Foundation, I'm able to give back in return for the bountiful life I've been given. My partner in the foundation, my wife Janet, works with me to choose recipients. Recently, we dedicated funds to Ethiopian famine relief, a homeless shelter in Rhode Island, and a church-based mentoring program in New London, Connecticut. I'd like to make a point here about business and profit networking through charitable volunteerism. It happens all the time and is a good way for some to make money while making charitable contributions. In this situation, however, if I receive new business as a result of the foundation, I reinvest the proceeds into the program.

The mentoring program we fund assists children from homes fraught with domestic violence, substance abuse, parental neglect—you name it. The mentoring program provides these kids with a safe haven, food, and homework help after school. But they also get something far more valuable. The mentors teach them the value of living a life of honesty and integrity. They find the kinds of positive human qualities they might not see at home, and that's why I knew we had to help financially. The program is run by the church's minister, a client of mine who told me about the wonderful changes the program makes in young lives—lives otherwise left to horrid conditions and tragically predictable results.

An important part of the foundation is extending loans without an expectation of repayment. Our inspiration comes in part from Nobel Peace Prize–winner Muhammad Yunus, who fosters economic and social development by creating loans for the poor. His Bangladesh-based Grameen Bank loans are small, but they make a huge difference to the borrower. For example, the loan might be enough to purchase some seed for a plot of land or a well pump to nourish a drought-stricken village back to life. The most amazing part is the astonishing integrity of some of the borrowers. The borrowers, poor as they may be, have shown a surprising tendency to repay the loans. They understand the concept of financial accountability far better than many Americans, and they have learned to save and protect what little they have. (In my business, I sometimes cite these borrowers when trying to illustrate the value of financial prudence and discipline to potential retirees.)

Inspired by the Grameen Bank program, Janet and I do the same sort of thing on a more local basis. We set up a loan program with a repayment schedule but no fees, penalties, or payment deadlines. In short, we have no expectation of being repaid. For us, it's all about touching lives. If these small loans help recipients make better life decisions, that's payment enough.

A surprising number of our American borrowers have shown a determination to repay the loans. Given the chance to prosper, they respond with newfound dignity to manage their credit more effectively. And even if they never repay, we're happy to help them through the tough times.

How is this related to the business of financial planning and safe-retirement advocacy? For one, it keeps me in touch with the spirit of helping, instead of just taking—more profit, more clientele, and more industry influence. None of those impulses are necessarily wrong, but without a renewed inspiration to help everyone we touch and remain accountable in everything we do, businesspeople sometimes lose sight of the way to really succeed inside and outside the workplace.

Out of the office and away from the business world, the same spirit creates a strong community of loyal friends, neighbors, and family members. Let's face it, there have been, and will certainly be, times when this kind of soul investment becomes more important than anything money can buy. We all know that, but practice puts meaning into the process.

Selling by Not Selling

Strangely enough, to excel in sales I decided not to sell, not in the "selling" sense of the word. I know this sounds like an oxymoron—what could I possibly mean by saying I excel in sales by not selling?

My sales arise from the development of relationships, rather than from pressure sales and persuasion techniques. It means everything to me to get to know you. The rest just naturally falls into place because we have a relationship. I know you, and you know me. We work together to create the very best plan for you. It's not about selling you something. You consider the undeniable facts—all of them—

and make your own informed decisions about having guaranteed security in your retirement. Non-selling, fact finding, income-based retirement planning—that's me. In the end, I feel great about what we've done, and I get paid for it. What could be better?

If you think selling is all about attitude, you're right. But it's also about investing yourself into relationships with your clients. You have to feel and believe in the needs of other people. Oh, and you have to love people. I have seen an amazing number of people trying to sell products of all kinds, without really being "people people." You know what I mean: everyone's encountered a salesperson who constantly projects the message, "I hate my job, I hate being here, and I am miserable." That attitude is sure to make customers miserable, too, until they walk out the door, probably without buying anything.

I challenge insurance companies to help themselves by creating products that help consumers realize their needs in every way possible. This will help the company's agents foster better relationships with the people they serve. I continue to see a need in the insurance business for a reconciliation between the needs of companies and their clients. Many companies still don't get it. If you offer better products and services, more people will choose to buy insurance products rather than products from riskier areas of the financial arena.

Insurance versus the Market

I know I've given the industry a bit of a drubbing, so let me say for the record that insurance products have come a long way—for the better—in the past thirty years. A wealth of improvements has affected not only the products we sell but also how we present them. I understand the critics of my industry. I know what motivates that criticism, so I know how to communicate with our critics. It's my understanding of that criticism that makes me a true safe-retirement advocate. Consider the following example.

I once met a couple who had done well in the bull market of the late 1990s, which had been full of seemingly unstoppable opportunities. Worth $500,000 on paper by the end of that period, the couple thought they had it all, including shares of WorldCom and Enron.

Of course, those names haunt us now, but at the time, they were some of the biggest names in the global market.

The rest is history. Enron collapsed in what we now see as one of the most heinous financial scandals in history. The fate of World-Com wasn't much better, and these mercurial stars burned out before the real 9/11-related market debacle began in earnest.

By the time I met this couple, circa 2000, their $500,000 nest egg had withered to $125,000 nearly overnight. They had heard about me, so they came to me for help. I'm glad they did, because we were able to make some smart, safe moves to secure their remaining assets before the real "market adjustment" became the full-blown crash. By then, they had learned their lessons well and were determined to forever avoid risk-related speculation. Had they waited to secure their funds against the rampant losses sparked by poor investment advice, this couple might have lost everything. Some planners had urged them to hang on, assuring them that they would make it all back one day.

Before I could make changes for them, we had to sit down and begin to build a trusting relationship. That began with an overall discussion about their wants and needs—beyond recapturing that evaporated $500,000 principal, of course. The rules were dramatically different from 2000 onward, and they have been changing by the day ever since.

- Rule One: The Roaring Nineties were over.
- Rule Two: Accept the reality of Rule One and shift certain assets into a safe, reliable source of guaranteed income.
- Rule Three: Forget those old dreams of greed, get out of risk, and begin to build again with a solid basis in guaranteed principal and income. Remember my conversion from Top Gun to seaside dweller? It's the same sort of thing.

It was a difficult era in many ways. The do-no-wrong frenzy of the 1990s had come to an end. Many people refused to believe it. Some blue-sky analysts called the "downturn" a market "hiccup." And of course, none of us had a clue about the coming 9/11 disaster. In the days after 9/11, the Twin Towers were still smoldering and market panic was running at full tilt. Yet many believed that the terrified flock on Wall Street would eventually settle down, people would come to their senses, and market shares and indices would stop plummeting at such a rapid rate. I think we were all a little stunned to experience the 1920s all over again.

Unfortunately, some of us don't seem to remember at all. For some people, it's as if it never happened. In 2006 and 2007, the stock market raced higher than ever before. Then came yet another beginning-of-the-bullish-end, as we quickly slid into the market fiasco of 2008. Once again, people lost a lot of money!

If you want to plan a successful retirement, you must be a maverick. You must buck the trend to hop the fast-gain gravy train. You must also understand that the Roaring Nineties and the post-9/11 bounce are over, and that betting on the constant promise of an 11 percent historic market return is not a sound retirement plan. Any good planner will tell you that, and there are many good people in this business.

A friend recently told me that his circa-2000 portfolio lost $1,000,000, or more than 60 percent of its value. He'd been pumped full of market wisdoms of the day: buy and hold, buy low and sell high, go for solid-growth companies with strong earnings, and of course the big one—*accept the risk of periodic loss in order to gain the 11 to 12 percent historical return.* He bought right, held tight, and made a fortune on paper. Then he began to lose. Still holding on for dear life, he and his planner failed to anticipate the decline ahead— just like everyone else. So he and his fellow buy-and-hold diehards kept on holding, all the way to the bottom. Fortunately, my friend had purchased his assets in the 1980s, well before the market frenzy of the 1990s. He'd lost a million dollars on paper, but he hadn't lost much of his original principal—only his exorbitant profits.

He started over at square one, building steadily and prudently, and shoring up his risk portfolio with guaranteed income and principal-preserving instruments. Now, he can retire in comfort, but he still hasn't recovered emotionally. When he tells his story, his eyes reveal the hurt and dismay. The buy-and-hold mantra of the era let him down, and he can't help but suspect certain market analysts in the media. Speculating about when we'll "find the top or bottom of the market," they still talk the same talk. Back then, as now, who knew exactly whom to trust for an accurate forecast? Is a truly accurate financial/economic forecast even possible when an emotional trigger—another terrorism incident, for example—could send the market into another unexpected tailspin?

Many other investors weren't so fortunate. Most who lost money in the crash bought in the 1990s, so they lost a lot of hard-earned cash. Today, however, I don't think people would hang on so long. Even if you look at the performance of Warren Buffett's Berkshire Hathaway from 1998 to 2008, you wouldn't have an accurate picture of Berkshire Hathaway shares in 1997. Even if you factor in Buffett's financial wizardry, Berkshire values in 1997 were strongly influenced by the hard-charging 1990s overall.

Would a ten-year Berkshire extrapolation made today carry an accurate picture of the coming ten years? If you study the company's value over long periods of time, Berkshire Hathaway has been successful. But consider the ten-year cyclical success formula with this example. The year is 1999. Let's say you've invested heavily in Warren Buffett's Berkshire Hathaway, and you're excited about retirement. You're ready to retire—in fact, you're counting the days. In March 1999, your Berkshire Hathaway stock closes at $80,000, and you feel like you're in great financial shape.

Then a sudden market "adjustment" begins to gather momentum. The Berkshire stock begins to slide. "No problem," you say, and you stick to your guns and the ten-year plan. A few months go by as you wait for some improvement, but by March 2000, your Berkshire shares close at $41,000. Berkshire has lost nearly half its value, and you're beginning to wonder when to retire. Perhaps some interim consulting work might be in order, as you wait for your shares to recover.

Next comes the 9/11 pandemonium. It will be another three and a half years before Berkshire Hathaway returns to $80,000.

After that, we were in a more bullish market for a time, and Berkshire produced a steady 7.5 percent annual return—only slightly beating overall market gains. And this was an investment managed by one of the greatest investment minds of our lifetime.

Let's return to the example of the Berkshire Hathaway investment you made in 2000. Now let's say you were sixty-five at the time.

Could you wait another six years to retire? Given the loss of that single investment—even an investment managed by a great financial mind—would your other assets fare as well? If the Berkshire shares were your only losses, would you still have to wait for recovery before retiring?

In an upside scenario, while wanting to remain an active player in the marketplace, he might have put some of his money into a safe, income-producing instrument like an annuity. The annuity would have guaranteed both his principal and enough income to allow him to comfortably wait for the recovery of his Berkshire shares. He wouldn't necessarily be living like a prince, but his guaranteed income stream would allow him to retire at sixty-five, at a time when company headhunters were looking for younger talent to take his place at XYZ Corp.

In 2000, it was routine to hear about people losing 70 percent, 80 percent, and even 90 percent of their portfolios. Even some well-managed portfolios held steady losses in the 10 to 30 percent range. Why such a disparity of results when the hammer came down? Think about it: some investors had better advice than others. Some were vested in instruments other than stock, bonds, and real estate. Some were already into guaranteed income vehicles, so they cruised through the crash relatively unscathed. So what about you? What kind of diversity is in your portfolio? What does diversity mean to your financial advisor? Does it include guaranteed income for life? This particular financial climate requires a safety measure or two.

I once met a man in Rhode Island who had a mutual-fund portfolio worth roughly $500,000. He'd been with a broker for several years who favored mutual funds, and he was able to withdraw around 10 percent a year—$56,000 a year, to be exact. His funds had been steadily going up 10 percent a year, so he didn't have to dig into his principal. He was living a wonderful life, having fun and playing golf, until he hit the wall along with everyone else in 2001.

His portfolio dropped like a rock almost overnight, to $260,000. In order to maintain his $56,000 annual income, he would have to withdraw 21 percent each year—a hazardous depletion of his resources, because 21 percent returns were nearly impossible to come by. When he asked me for advice, I suggested he take out $13,000 a year because returns were in the tank across the board. He didn't want to hear that. He wanted to hear about ways to make 10 to 13 percent on his money without fear of losing more principal.

I let him walk out of my office and look for another planner. He was in serious denial, as were many others at the time, and reality forced him to go back to work. The tragedy is that it didn't have to happen that way. Had he used a safe-retirement advocate from the beginning, he would have built some kind of safety net into his portfolio. He would have been able to wait for the recovery of his mutual-fund portfolio in relative style.

But in the boom times, when upside potential seems to have no end, some people actually see risk in diverting a single dollar away from speculative investments. The human mind can be a strange thing to watch. Immersed in the spiraling momentum of greed, we lose all fear until we learn the lesson of temperance. That lesson comes by stealth in the murky atmosphere of human error, mixed market signals, and conflicting economic data.

An appropriately tempered financial portfolio is the safest form of financial protection you will ever find. Since my earliest beginnings in this business, more than thirty years ago, I knew I would have to guide my clients through rough waters. I'd heard every story about the great crash of 1929, and I was determined to prepare myself, and my clients, for the worst. I learned the value of safe-haven planning. I look back at everything I've done in my life—from the shoe store, to the summer camp, to my beginnings in the insurance business, to real estate, and even to motel ownership—and in the end, I returned to what I knew best.

After some of the worst market declines in our lifetime, my retired clients have been able to recover their losses without having to go back to work. To some readers, that might sound a bit flat—as if such an accomplishment could be had by anyone. But having read this chapter, you know the truth. It was the result of solid, truly historically based, and mathematically driven common sense. I'm no Einstein. I simply persuaded my clients to acquire some guaranteed income through annuities.

CHAPTER 8

The Intimate Art of Goal Tending:
Finding Out What Really Matters

Has your advisor *really* probed your life goals, other than your financial ones? If not, it might be unintentional, as your planner might have missed the opportunity to get to know you and establish a relationship. If so, I suggest you start now and establish the same kind of rapport with your planner that you have with people who really know you. Share your life goals with your planner and define who you really are.

Before launching into a discussion of goals and motivations, let me say that I am not opposed to other kinds of investments, including mutual funds, individual stocks and bonds, real estate, and all the rest. They all have a place in certain financial strategies. But the primary goal for my clients is to reach both a practical and strategic result containing certain guarantees that come from implementing a practical, mathematically driven process designed to ensure peace of mind in retirement. That's it. I make sure such methods continue to add a certain degree of earnings to a client's asset base, but I am not in the business of making anyone rich. My goal in business is to keep your riches intact.

As I've illustrated in previous chapters of this book, the preservation of assets should be a simple matter. If you act early enough and do the right things in advance—and even if you implement safe-retirement strategies during your retirement—you can achieve guaranteed assets and income. But we've seen some tricky variables at work, including greed, fear, and even panic. In short, let emotion run wild, and all bets are off as an emotional wild card wreaks havoc with your financial deck of cards.

To best manage this wild card, never wait until hard times come to do the right thing. Balance your portfolio with common-sense instruments of asset preservation, and do it when times are good, when your investment strategy is running predictably and your emotions are stabilized. However, if you happen to be reading this book during a period of economic upheaval, the same rule holds true, perhaps even more so—take a percentage of your earnings and set them aside in safe-harbor instruments.

Simple, right? It would be, if not for the most overlooked, underestimated aspect of the financial planning process, and I am *not* talking about the money. I'm talking about the essential message of this chapter, which confronts the nemesis of nearly every investor on the planet—the "E word," emotion.

Peace of Mind through Self-Acceptance

We'll talk more about asset preservation in a moment, but first let's talk about a major, yet more subtle, emotional inhibitor: worry. Fear is one kind of emotion and worry is yet another—a modified version of fear in which we ponder the minutiae of financial details. Let's face it, most of us worry about our money, but we don't really think about it in a fully rational sense. We worry about how to make more, how to keep what we have, and what to do with the money we hope to pass on to others. Worry is a less precise emotion that is driven by a flurry of sometimes nebulous factors, all of which create a general uneasiness instead of efficient, workable results. In short, formless worry tends to undermine logical, productive financial thinking, which inhibits well-founded, proactive decision making. And that has cost many an investor his retirement lifestyle, especially in recent years.

For some people, worry is an ongoing, nagging state of mind. It may be shoved into the subconscious for a time, but it often bubbles to the surface when we try to enjoy a serene moment, a conversation with a friend, or a balanced look at a financial portfolio.

Any good financial planner, therefore, seeks to achieve a degree of success in helping others reach their financial goals without worry. The cliché "worry free" is tossed about a good deal in my business, but think about it in the "real time" of your own existence. Have you ever really been worry free? For many, this would be a new level of emotional stability, a cathartic revelation of clarity. Truly worry-free people begin to see and hear the world in different ways. They're suddenly tuned in to new levels of valuation and life priorities—which tend to inspire new levels of loyalty toward safe-retirement planning, by the way—but some people never get there. Instead, they remain shackled to every blip on the market indices. They never know the calm of income guarantees in retirement, safety of principal, or overall asset preservation.

Each time I have the privilege to see a client achieve a relative level of calm, I want to do it again and again for others. Annuity professionals sleep well at night knowing our clients will never wake up to an emotionally devastating TV news report about another crash on the Dow, NASDAQ, or S&P, even if the client might have chosen to maintain some level of market exposure.

Yet for some, terms like "calm" and "peace of mind" have no tactile or experiential meaning. These people never seem to have enough money and instead pursue relentless efforts to get more—until the bottom drops out and they come to people like me to make miracles happen. Sometimes, I am able to give such clients peace of mind and enable them to move forward and grow their portfolios in repair mode, but they're often required to scale back their expectations. We all live in the real world, but some of us don't know it until it's too late. Some live in a cultural fantasy driven by risk, including excessive spending, speculative investment based on groundless hearsay (which often fuels the trading, in my opinion), credit-card debt, and other financial calamities.

This cultural fantasy is a personal environment filled with things people think they have to have in order to be happy. These imaginary needs are culturally assimilated through movies, TV shows, and a relentless river of print advertisements, commercials, and other marketing imagery that define a fantasy world of success. Some of us imagine we must have these things to be accepted, keep our friends, and maintain the respect of our neighbors and family members. In some social circles, the sad little rule of widget-based acceptance may be true, but it's also a mind trick. In recent years, many people in this environment have been forced by market conditions to adjust their minds to new lifestyles, and they've learned something along the way—they don't need all that stuff.

So, here's the bottom line, according to Reindel: The secret for many people living successfully in retirement is simply accepting who they are. They no longer think they have to compete in a materialistic fantasy world. They no longer have to play according to the rules of the very latest trends in business attire, which is often a necessary component of the working world. They do not see the need to possess the latest electronic gizmo or dine in expensive gourmet restaurants. But they do live well, because they were able to change their thinking through an often overlooked aspect of retirement planning: I call it emotional perspective.

We may need to achieve happiness and peace of mind in a place where a good pre-owned car and a slightly dated kitchen leave room for other pursuits, such as frequent travel to see friends, family members, and distant destinations. Retirement planning therefore benefits from breaking the ball-and-chain of envy.

Some people follow every trend in fashion and decor for fear of looking dated. This can be especially true in our working years, when some of us feel like slaves to trends, often tossing out perfectly good, working appliances to repurchase the same appliances in a shiny new wrapper (which will also look dated in a few years). Landfills across America are filled with the chains of fashion. To break those chains, some of us will have to tear up credit cards and take more responsibility for the incidental items we buy on a daily basis.

As I age, this has become one of my most important goals. It means separating myself from old habits and desires and adjusting my own expectations to focus more on what I have now and who I am in the present. That brings me to the issue of health and living in the moment of who we are, both physically and financially.

It's all about perception. Physical fitness is equally vital as we age. Yet for certain people, advancing age is nothing but a frustrating process of comparing themselves to the robust athletes they once were in their teens and twenties. Instead of maintaining a happy, healthy regimen of diet and exercise, they give up in despair and ruminate about the physical past they think they've lost.

This often translates into the financial realm as well. Some of us simply throw our arms up in resignation and accept the free-form profit-and-loss cycles of Wall Street instead of preserving and enjoying the presence of financial stability we may already have. Again, it's all about perception.

But not everyone manages to make this paradigm shift in value perception. I don't know how many times I've seen people in the midst of a perfectly balanced retirement blow it all on an impulse. They have what they need at first: a good income stream, friends, health, hobbies, and travel. Suddenly, a friend brags about getting a big windfall from a hot stock, and they're right back in it all over again, ready to speculate. This is where seniors often fall prey to unscrupulous opportunists. Some of these opportunists are financial analysts who criticize safe-haven investment vehicles in favor of risk. Suddenly, financial balance is lost, and along with it goes that peace of mind.

I say this because it's important to recognize now what will be most important to you in the future. Realize the essentials of your own hopes and dreams, and not the fantasy standards of society. Ask yourself where you would like to be in retirement, both intellectually and emotionally, with a balanced sense of material need. Most people don't think about planning for the less tangible, more emotionally driven part of our true selves, which we'll inevitably encounter one day. But failing to adjust a financial plan to accommodate the needs of your true self in the future, and the fluctuating nature of market economies, can trigger unwise financial decisions and dissatisfaction.

Some mature adults never entirely escape this comparative mentality in their senior years; as a result, they may never fully realize happiness, whether they lose their money through excessive risk or not. Some fail to live in the now of adequate financial security, even as they hold it—however temporarily—in their hands.

How many times have you heard about seniors being duped into participating in a dangerously risky investment scheme? Why would seniors take such a chance if they had everything they needed? Probably because they had no idea how to get what they weren't sure they really wanted in the first place. Some people retain those fears, no matter what a financial planner may explain to them from an intellectual or philosophical standpoint. At an advanced age, some fail to see the statistical peril of taking additional risk, and it's no joke when a senior accordingly loses a significant chunk of her nest egg by following the pitch of an ill-informed relative or unscrupulous salesperson.

Early on, I recognized the financial perils of this kind of emotional trap. I try to be a spiritual being in the physical world, always prepared to face head-on any material lessons in the here and now. I still learn as I go, which makes the reality of my own guaranteed retirement income all the more important. My own resulting peace of mind allows me to grow spiritually, without the nagging worries about material survival at every turn. Thanks to my own safe-retirement portfolio, I have more time to get to know myself and others around me. I've created enough emotional room to be comfortable with myself as the pace of my physical body begins to slow down; hopefully, when I reach old age, I will be happy with who I am, give or take a few bumps and bruises along the way.

If this sounds like ethereal thinking to you, think again. It is actually the most critical component of traditional financial planning, because your thinking processes will likely slow with your physical abilities. When that happens, you will become more vulnerable to a formless sense of personal dissatisfaction, which can lead to financial disaster. Your spiritual life and your intellect can keep your emotions in check, keeping you from overreacting when the rest of the financial world is in a temporary tizzy.

No Time for Games

I've also learned to quit playing games. Candor and honesty have become an intrinsic part of me and who I am. My wife, children, and parents mean the world to me, but unfortunately, that's not the case in every family. Game playing in families can lead to terrible emotional angst and financial errors.

Sometimes, aging parents try to make themselves more important in the lives of their children by gifting—or withholding—money. People nearing or just entering retirement must carefully define their own goals for gifting and inheritance. Make sure your goals are your own, and not those of your children or grandchildren. Next, make sure that your children are aware of your plans early on, and stay true to those goals—and yourself. To do so, you have to enter the emotional, intellectual, and spiritual realm of your own perceptions, which dictate the way you think about and act upon your financial future. Finding your financial self can be difficult.

In the world of dollars, common sense, political turmoil, and related emotional effects on market indices, seniors who control significant amounts of money must monitor, study, and continue to learn about the latest investments and strategies. Seniors in charge of estates must also remain immune to the emotional and tactical lures of financial marketing—which is exactly why it's a good idea to place a certain amount of assets in guaranteed-income instruments early on.

On a Personal Note

Financial planners must deal with irrational emotions in this business, regardless of the client's age. At any age, emotions can make or break financial destinies. The better prepared we are individually, emotionally, and even spiritually, the better off we'll be in the pinch of an economic downturn. Personally, I feel that I am prepared for anything. I am happy and spiritually centered, but it didn't happen without the help of some very special people.

My stepfather has long been a guiding force in my life. He taught me the honest work ethic that drove me to believe in, and implement, the business values I have today. He was the first to convince me that I would have to make my own way in life, and those essential values formed the future I enjoy today. My stepfather also taught me about how to treat others ethically and how to conduct fair and honest business transactions; his rock-solid personal ethics translated to the way he treated me, my mother, and his own mother.

I wanted to give something back to him and my mother, and after a lot of hard work, I was finally able to do just that. I bought my parents a house seven miles away from my own home, and I am able to support them in their retirement. Today, they are living a wonderful retirement lifestyle, and I am living a wonderful life as a result of the upbringing they gave me. I hope I've passed on to you some of the same lessons my stepfather taught me.

CHAPTER 9

The Way I Do Business

THE SIZE OF YOUR ASSET PORTFOLIO IS IMMATERIAL TO ME. Whether you have $2,000, or $2 million, doesn't matter at all. For one client, I recently moved $2,000 out of a CD that paid out only 1 percent and put the money into an annuity that paid 3 percent. It took as much time as it would take me to transfer $2 million from a CD to an annuity, but for this effort I made only $50. Yet the $2,000 move was as important to that particular client as a $2 million transfer would have been to another.

For another client and his wife, I designed an income plan involving $100,000. After drawing income from the plan for a period of time, the client found that he needed to retrieve some principal to address certain health problems. Because of the way I had positioned their money, he was able to retrieve the principal he and his wife needed without incurring penalties. Due to unavoidable changes in their lives, the retrieval was necessary, and the plan was flexible enough to allow them to do what they needed to do to live in comfort and with peace of mind.

If you have your portfolio with a seasoned client advocate, you will likely see this type of work ethic. It all comes down to credibility. A lot of that credibility has much to do with the way advisors feel about themselves, which in turn affects the client's feelings about the advisor after they do business together. Credible advisors deal in truths, not half-truths; half-truths lead to confusion, disappointment, and perhaps even disgruntled customers. If all advisors understood this, our industry would be much better off as a whole.

Back to the couple who needed to withdraw principal to address health expenses. I was frank with them about their decision, letting them know that early withdrawal would shorten the length of time their money would last. Not all planners are willing to do what I did, but it's part of my own personal philosophy of life. I believe that what comes around, goes around. There are hard facts that people need to consider when making their retirement plans, and any planner worth his salt should make you aware of all of them:

- Long-term care must be addressed in your retirement plan, and traditional insurance is not the only answer. Most people only think about long-term care when they are in "crisis mode," which is unnecessary and unfortunate. Lack of advance planning can put you in grave financial peril.
- You must be realistic about what you can expect your assets to return. Most people have totally unrealistic expectations.
- You must think differently about money and lifestyles after retirement.
- You must understand safe-haven investments, including certain types of annuities, and how they work. Annuities as a whole have been unfairly criticized for politically motivated purposes, and even as I write this, a war is being waged in the financial world to capture the retirement portfolios of baby boomers.
- Government and corporate leaders have little interest in the financial welfare of retired individuals. In fact, they are currently taking direct action to divest themselves of that responsibility. You must take responsibility for your own life and financial future.
- You must educate yourself as much as possible about financial instruments of all kinds.
- You do not need to earn 70 to 100 percent of your preretirement income each year to have a happy, secure retirement. This is a complete myth.

It is no myth, however, that failure to realize these factors may put you in peril. All it takes is a minor glitch in the economy to put company profits and employment into a tailspin. For example, a major drug company recently had a problem with the development of a blockbuster drug. The drug, an anticholesterol medication, caused high blood pressure in some test patients. After years of research and millions of dollars, the company did the right thing and cancelled production of the medication, which caused a cataclysmic drop in its stock price. Employees' emotions ran the gamut. Among the various panic-mode reactions were taking early retirement and dumping their own shares of company stock.

Another example occurred at an engineering firm. A major defense contractor and one of only two U.S. companies designing and building nuclear submarines, the firm was largely dependent on Navy contracts that were in turn dependent on waging and winning internal political battles over the cost and use of various facilities. As a result, workers remained in a constant state of anxiety.

The average worker at this particular engineering firm was older than most workers in other firms, and as many of them neared retirement, the company decided to change its pension program to a "cash-balance" plan. I'll spare you the details here, but let it suffice to say that the switch had a dramatic effect on employee retirement scenarios.

On top of that, there was the significant factor of the whims of the military. The home port for East Coast–based nuclear submarine operations was located only a few miles away from the firm's headquarters. Although it might seem that having such a powerful and important operation so close by would make employees feel more secure about keeping the military's business, it wasn't so—during a ten-year period, the base had been slated for closure twice. Both times, local, state, and regional governments waged political battles to save the base, but it still remained a prime target for politicians wanting to cut pork from the budget. A major part of the local government's strategy to save the base was to emphasize its proximity to the engineering firm, which employed thousands of workers. Talk about uncertainty!

My basic message is this: there is no guaranteed security other than guaranteed income from specific investment instruments. I know I can make a difference by sending this broad-based message across the nation: I can help you define and solve financial uncertainties, and make sure you have the information you need to address those uncertainties and select appropriate alternatives to fit your retirement plan.

But remember, competition is fierce in the financial world. People in the financial industry have been playing hardball, spreading disinformation about competing products and sectors in the financial arena. Some will tell you that all annuities are bad because they offer conservative returns as opposed to the meteoric short-term gains made possible with high-risk investments. Well, of course annuities offer conservative returns! Annuities aren't really investments—they are savings instruments that offer safe harbor for principal, and they provide a steady, dependable, and guaranteed income stream.

The Importance of Liquidity

Certain gurus will tell you to avoid annuities because you can't gain instant access to all of your money at once—for example, if you have an impulsive need to jump on one of their hot stock tips. But why would you want to do that? As of this writing, world securities markets and major global financial institutions are experiencing unprecedented volatility. The U.S. government has been forced to provide massive amounts of money to bail out the entire financial system. But somehow, incredibly, certain analysts and traders continue to insist that setting aside principal in a safe-haven instrument to generate guaranteed income is somehow a bad thing.

Of course, you may need instant liquidity in some situations, and certain people will tell you that annuities offer lots of liquidity. But here's the truth: liquidity means immediate access to cash. Annuity salespeople love to point to the "liquidity options" offered with various annuity packages, which has sparked a firestorm of criticism from insurance industry regulators and media pundits alike. Make sure when considering the purchase of an annuity that you are aware of all the liquidity options the annuity offers in the event of an emergency.

Most carriers allow you to withdraw 10 percent of your accumulated value per year without incurring a penalty. Some may offer more, and the same contract also might allow the withdrawal of

100 percent of value, penalty free, if the contract owner becomes confined to a nursing home for sixty or more consecutive days. For example, one policy offers 100 percent liquidity in the event of the diagnosis of terminal illness, and a 20 percent withdrawal provision for home health care. That's a fairly generous liquidity option compared with other products.

On the other hand, a competing ten-year annuity allows little more than the standard 10 percent annual withdrawal of the annuity's total, accumulated value, with no more than 20 percent available penalty free after a full ninety days of consecutive confinement in a nursing home. And here's another point: does the annuity you're considering offer a 10 percent penalty-free withdrawal of the total accumulated value of the contract, meaning principal plus earnings? Or is the allotted withdrawal limited to principal alone?

One seven-year annuity allows a 10 percent penalty-free withdrawal beginning in the first year, but not all do. Although this particular annuity does offer 100 percent liquidity for bedridden nursing-home patients (again after ninety consecutive days), it restricts terminal-illness withdrawals to only 25 percent of the account's total accumulated value. In the event of the untimely demise of a contract owner, a good annuity's carrier would still have a continuing payout obligation; just about every annuity contract in deferral should allow the named beneficiary to receive the remaining contract value. But again, you should look for this kind of information in the "death benefits" section of any consumer brochures or contracts.

Other liquidity options include annuities limited to a 3 percent immediate interest withdrawal during the contract's first year, followed by annual 10 percent penalty-free withdrawals after that. Here again, you should consider the benefits of the overall package, but you can see that a list of liquidity options may not equate to real liquidity, unless you find yourself near death or confined to a nursing home.

Liquidity remains a critical consideration when shopping annuities, and without prior knowledge of the array of liquidity variables in the fixed-annuity marketplace, it's nearly impossible to comparison shop. After reading this book, you now know where to begin.

Annuities must be shopped carefully to maximize liquidity, but keep in mind that you will probably have to sacrifice gains to maintain liquidity. It will be hard to find an annuity that promises 10 percent gains and total liquidity. If you want to stay in the game for that kind of gain, have at it in the market: some people love to gamble for the sheer adrenaline thrill of it. But make sure you have insured enough principal as a safety net for the many times the market will take yet another dive, because this will be part of our reality for years to come.

A Message to Fellow Boomers

Like many nearing retirement, I, too, am a baby boomer. I'm near the front of the line of boomer retirees, but we all share the same experiences: the tumultuous cultural, economic, and political turmoil of the 1960s, 1970s, and 1980s. We've been in it together from Vietnam all the way to 9/11, and now we head into retirement sharing a mindset of common values.

It is no coincidence that one popular financial firm chose *Easy Rider* star Dennis Hopper to promote its retirement products. In one commercial, Hopper declares that our generation will "blow the lid off" traditional retirement styles. Do you think you'll "blow the lid off" retirement? Soon after that commercial began to air, something surely blew the lid off portfolio loss rates, and today, most of the people I talk to from our generation are quite worried about retirement. We aren't thinking about hang gliding—we're fretting about hanging on financially in our declining years. Given inflation, market uncertainties, terrorism, and general economic/political instability around the globe, we worry about the future.

To ensure that you safely navigate these troubled times, you must be at the helm of your own destiny. You need to think of yourself as an independent entity capable of calling your own shots in the financial arena, which means establishing a certain base level of guaranteed financial independence. I want to help you do that through insurance-based financial planning. In this market, at this time in our history, insurance-based planning remains a controversial concept, but I firmly believe a trend in insurance-based planning is long overdue. Other planners may have different ideas about tackling the problem of guaranteed income, but I believe insurance-based planning is the only way to get the job done.

The way I do business today is akin to financial detox. Some of my clients come to me with an addiction to certain types of financial risk. Although they're hesitant to spare a single dollar currently invested in risk-related speculation, they have become believers of insurance-based planning. Annuities can guarantee the peace of mind you get from knowing that fundamental costs of living, like health care and property taxes, are covered.

You do not need 70 to 100 percent of your preretirement income to be happy in retirement. People in financial services, stocks, and bonds love to tell you otherwise because they stand to gain by giving you that advice. They want you to keep working so you can buy more products with empty promises of 10 to 12 percent returns. But the only way to really understand your retirement-income need is to make a budget based on what you spend now, away from work. Since you won't be working, for example, you won't have the costs related to keeping pace with others in the workplace. You won't need the money associated with commuting costs, wardrobe, and other image-related items. You won't have the same income needs if your mortgage is paid off, and if you rely on the 70 to 100 percent rule of thumb, you might be way off altogether.

CHAPTER 10

Ideal Clients Plan Less Risk

A T WHAT MOMENT SHOULD WE BEGIN TO SHIFT AWAY FROM risk and move toward security? As previously suggested on page 69, the ideal time to shift from market risk to safe-harbor instruments, such as annuities, might begin around the age of fifty-five (or even sixty-five, considering increasing life expectancies and other factors). People focused on an earlier retirement could even consider such a shift in their mid-forties.

For younger people, however, even the moderation of market exposure available with a variable annuity is not always an obvious choice. Direct market exposure with stocks and bonds makes more sense for younger investors because they are in the height of their earning years. They have time enough to recover from losses in the stock market and may not need the variable or fixed annuity's additional promise of future income and tax-deferred earnings. However, it wouldn't be unwise for anyone to move a small piece of his or her portfolio into some kind of fixed annuity in case an accident, illness, or other event results in unemployment.

For the most part, other instruments, such as IRAs and employer-sponsored 401(k) plans (some of which also provide tax-deferred growth and other advantages) make more sense for younger investors. For these investors, it is prudent to maximize IRA or 401(k) contributions before investing in variable annuities, primarily because variable annuities provide no upfront tax advantages. Variables often have other desirable features, including death benefit protection and lifetime income payments, but their taxable status can be quite complex. If you are considering a purchase, first visit a qualified tax professional to get all the facts.

It takes a special client to appreciate the crucial need for guaranteed income and asset preservation. I wish more people would see the light early on, but many of my clients have already been around the block by the time they come to me. As a result, they've achieved a place in life where they've become more conservative and risk averse. They want peace of mind, and they're fed up with the erosion of their assets.

Many of these people have gained this wisdom through bad experiences with various planners and advisors. They've dealt with insurance agents who were complacent or didn't care or with securities dealers who advocated more risk than the client cared to take. They are well-read and now weigh their own opinions, based on past experience, right alongside those of the advisors they consult. They know all about the perils of spending too many of their assets too soon, or not having enough to begin with. They're also more realistic about how much money they really need to live on, because they've already begun to change the way they think about retirement. With that perspective in mind, client and advisor get together and consider the various sources of income the client can count on: perhaps pensions, Social Security, IRAs, 401(k)s, and so on.

Savings Accounts and CDs

Most people first think of savings accounts and CDs when they consider alternative savings options, and either or both may indeed be the best instruments for a particular investor at a particular time. I have often cautioned my own clients, regardless of their age, to keep a liquid nest egg for emergencies equal to at least six months of household income.

Both savings accounts and CDs are ideal for this purpose because they have comparatively low to zero penalties and are FDIC insured up to $100,000. (If your emergency cash requirements exceed

$100,000, separate the cash into multiple accounts.) Otherwise, go for the front lines of liquidity at the bank. But do bear in mind that interest rates that lag behind inflation equate to significant loss of potential assets over time.

It has often been said, and rightfully so, that money-market funds are not necessarily the safe haven they might appear to be. The same can be said for credit union CDs and other conventional savings accounts. But during the recent bear market on Wall Street, a huge number of investors kept their money on the sidelines in money-market funds and other "safe" harbors.

Treasuries

In addition to the obvious safety guarantees of the FDIC, you might also consider U.S. government bonds, which are otherwise known as Treasury bonds (or just T-bonds). They are arguably one of the world's safest instruments. Once again, there's a trade-off for that safety: government bonds offer some of the lowest yields at maturity. Other bonds offer greater yields at maturity but carry higher risk ratios, and even government bonds come with a degree of risk—the future selling price of the bond will always be unpredictable, regardless of its historic stability. T-bonds are typically issued in thirty-year maturity cycles and pay out in the form of biannual interest payments.

In addition to T-bonds, the government offers Treasury bills (T-bills) and Treasury notes (T-notes) issued in $1,000 increments, although required minimum purchase amounts may be imposed, depending upon the category of this type of security. T-bonds mature after ten or more years; T-notes mature after two to ten years, and T-bills are more forgiving, with some maturing in a year or less.

Issued in three different schedules of maturity, T-bills may come to maturity after 364 days, 182 days, or 91 days. Every Monday, the Treasury Department auctions T-bills that mature in 91 days and 182 days. Three-hundred-sixty-four-day T-bills are sold at auction thirteen times annually, at four-week intervals. T-bill interest rates are set at every auction based on the amount bidders are willing to pay for them. T-bills are accordingly sold at discount rates; they are the only Treasury securities with that distinction.

T-notes are issued with ten-year, five-year, three-year, or two-year schedules of maturity. You have the option to buy ten-year notes at auction six times a year. Three-year notes are made available each quarter, and monthly auctions are held for two- and five-year notes. Bottom line: All T-notes pay out in the form of interest payments made twice a year.

While interest payments from Treasuries may be exempt from state and local taxes, they are not immune to federal taxation. In addition, redemption before maturity is prohibited, but they generally lack "call" provisions, which means that interest payments stop when bonds are "called." A call provision in an investment contract allows a bond holder to buy a stated number of security shares at a stated price on or before a specific date of expiration for such a purchase. (Note that prior to 1985, call provisions were attached to certain T-bonds, which may call for a degree of caution when you are shopping the secondary market for this type of security.)

I like the accessibility of Treasury securities; individual investors can buy them directly from the federal government at routinely held auctions that are open to the public. If individuals choose to buy directly, they may save on broker commissions, but they lose the pre-maturity flexibility of early redemption, which may be possible if the bonds are purchased from a broker. Thus, any early sales would have to take place in the secondary market and be handled by a licensed securities broker (who would draw a commission). For more information or to buy government bills, notes, or bonds directly, contact the U.S. Bureau of Public Debt, an agency of the U.S. Department of the Treasury.

Other Investment Vehicles

You may also consider short- and long-term municipal bonds, which carry all sorts of risk levels. Priced and sold according to ratings from Morningstar and other rating services, major cities depend on these investment vehicles to build anything from highway networks to airports and art museums. While they can be relatively sound investments, make no mistake—municipalities sometimes default on scheduled bond payments, causing bond ratings and values to drop accordingly.

As for real estate, unless investors are very knowledgeable about the buy-and-flip process—buying properties below market level, renovating them according to a formula that allows for a specific profit margin, and then "flipping" or selling at that profit level—real estate generally requires a long-term hold to achieve profitable results.

You've probably heard about miracle bargains purchased at "tax sales," or residential real-estate auctions held by state and local governments. These properties are seized by the government for overdue property tax payments. In most states, home owners have significant rights of redemption and lengthy redemption periods. Thus, properties that are "purchased" by paying the taxes due on them are subject to such redemption periods before the full title may be issued. If the original owner makes his overdue tax payments, thereby redeeming the property—many do—the tax-sale investor has been waiting months for her investment capital to be freed up. In the end, the investor usually ends up with only a small gain, from a government-dictated interest payment for essentially loaning overdue taxes to the tax debtor.

Owning rental properties can be profitable in the long run, netting a tidy, regular income and perhaps windfall profits later on down the line for the right investor. But any investor who has ever experienced the rental real-estate market will say the same thing: it takes patience, commitment, passion, and a complicated formula of savings, repairs, and additional expenses to achieve these goals.

The Hazards of Reverse Mortgages

The rising popularity of the "reverse mortgage" is another matter. This instrument has been a boon for some and a travesty for others. The reverse mortgage is usually available after a homeowner reaches a certain age (currently sixty-two). The reverse mortgage is a last-ditch move, something that should be considered only if you need the money to survive. With a reverse mortgage, the homeowner is allowed to live in the home until she dies after receiving one of a variety of payout options. Upon the homeowner's death, the mortgage must be paid, and any excess funds would go to the beneficiaries of the estate. Reverse mortgages can be very costly, so read the fine print carefully and proceed with extreme caution.

Consider this disturbing trend that has emerged in recent years in the reverse mortgage industry. In one case, a California woman in her mid-sixties was coaxed into receiving a lump-sum payout for her reverse mortgage, which the mortgage salesperson persuaded her to reinvest in a ten-year annuity. Soon enough, the homeowner found herself penniless in a home she no longer owned. She was forced to live on food stamps for the next ten years, hoping to live long enough to see an income when she reached her mid-seventies and the annuity finally matured.

So what's my opinion about reinvesting reverse-mortgage money into annuities? Don't do it! The reverse mortgage is typically a last-resort option to create an additional retirement income stream. It is not a means to an end for entering into new investments or long-term asset-preservation strategies.

Long-Term Care

You must also plan for catastrophic illness, which can wipe out everything you've saved. If you have any assets at all, Medicare will not cover LTC in a nursing home. Medicare will pay for the first hundred days of nursing-home care, even for people with assets, but you must become impoverished to qualify for state-funded care through Medicaid if you require ongoing nursing-home care.

Thus, if you've worked a lifetime to enjoy your retirement, you won't qualify for Medicaid, so your nursing-home care will be financed out of your own pocket unless you have LTC insurance. LTC insurance is so prohibitively expensive that most people shy away from it—and that's only if they can qualify for it at all, given their current health conditions.

As previously discussed, some people are surprised when they hear about the more cost-effective and accessible LTC alternatives included with certain annuities, which also provide income guarantees and preserve principal at the same time. But how can you be assured that your annuity principal, proceeds, and other types of insurance will remain safe for the long-term future? First, you should select insurance products with an "A" rating or above (A+, etc.).

Your State Insurance Department's Role

These instruments carry an excellent level of legal reserves, which are required and regulated by state insurance departments. Legal reserves are monies set aside to ensure the guaranteed safety of a purchaser's premium payments for, or a principal contribution to, an insurance product (see below for more details). Your state's insurance department or insurance regulatory commission accordingly supervises every aspect of an insurance company's operations within your state. These departments approve—and suspend or revoke—insurance licenses for companies and individual agents. Without a license, companies and agents are out of business, so you can imagine the clout your state's insurance department has over the industry. The departments also approve and regulate all insurance-policy forms and, in most states, even insurance companies' sales and marketing materials must be approved by the departments before being offered to the public. The departments review consumer complaints and company merger proposals, and they intervene in other aspects of the industry.

One of the regulatory department's most important responsibilities is to ensure and regulate the material integrity of your insurance policy's legal reserve, which is also known as the "reserve fund." A large percentage of each premium dollar collected by an insurance company will go into the policyholder's reserve fund, which is established as a way of measuring how much money a company must set aside to meet the future commitments of the policies it issues. In other words, reserve funds ensure that insurance companies will have enough assets to pay their claims and other commitments when they are due. The policy reserve fund is legally required by each state, and while it's a liability for insurance companies, it is an important financial safeguard put in place to make sure assets are kept intact for the payout of both living and death benefits to policyholders and their survivors. All life-insurance companies in compliance with state legal reserve requirements are known as "legal reserve" life-insurance companies. Thus, it is important that any annuity you consider should come from a legal reserve life-insurance company. Then you know the company is holding legal reserves to guarantee your principal.

Retirement Security

Over time, I've watched countless clients become very comfortable with the assets they have. No matter what products I recommend, my clients know they will have money deposited directly into their accounts on a monthly basis. They won't have to worry about the market, because they will never lose their principal investment if the market takes a momentary nosedive.

Now, if the economy suffered a string of five, six, or even seven bad years, some of my clients might see some effect on their overall retirement plan. Yet they would feel far less of an impact than someone with assets in the stock market. I'm further able to mitigate that impact by watching each portfolio very closely, using tools like my Safe-Retirement Incomer program, which, along with other valuable retirement planning tools, helps forecast retirement income using various models and performance requirements. To really gauge the ongoing success of an individual strategy, I monitor the rising or falling costs of a variety of factors, including health care, income, inflation, and taxes.

To plan for shortfalls and stay in the market without risking principal, I also recommend certain fixed-indexed annuities from time to time. When I do, I'm careful to tell clients these annuities may not perform to expectations every single time. Some clients believe that fixed-indexed annuities perform like securities on the open market, and that indexed returns will provide the same performance as securities while providing guaranteed income and preserving principal. Obviously, this cannot happen, or everyone would own fixed-indexed annuities. However, the fixed-indexed annuity will let a policyholder enjoy some benefits of a healthy stock market while always protecting principal.

How Commissions Work, and What to Expect from Your Financial Planner

As for commissions earned from the sale of fixed-indexed and other annuities, some people find it surprising that I get paid by the insurance companies at all. I do get paid for selling annuities, and I'm sometimes asked how annuity commissions are paid out to agents without costing the customer a dime of his principal. You may get a lot of evasive answers or simply an honest shrug, because many in the field aren't clear on commission payments, so here's how it works.

Each year, the insurance carrier works hard to earn money on its assets, which are based on client contributions to annuities. Let's say a client deposits $100,000 into a ten-year annuity. Once the assets are vested with the company, the insurance carrier may elect to buy bonds that match the ten-year maturity period of the client's annuity. In a perfect world, the insurance company will earn 6 percent per year on the bonds. After that, the insurance carrier will calculate its operating and administrative expenses, its own profitability, and the commissions that are paid to agents, all out of the proceeds of the bonds' earnings.

If such company costs run 2.5 percent per year, out of the total 6 percent per year earned from the bond investments, the remaining funds will go toward either crediting fixed interest to the annuity or, if the client chooses, purchasing options, which are used to credit the annuity contract. In this situation, the insurance carrier has about 3.5 percent of the 6 percent bond earnings to put to work for the client, and in certain cases the 3.5 percent is credited to the client's full premium if the client selects a "fixed crediting strategy." The agent may accordingly be paid from the carrier's "spread," or the sum of money between the company's bond earnings and what the company credits to the client's annuity contract.

In essence, agent commissions come from the insurance carrier's share of the interest earned from the bonds. The bonds are purchased with proceeds collected from customers who purchase annuities—but it should be noted that all of the client's principal must be guaranteed solvent and protected on behalf of the client by a

government-mandated "reserve fund." Although this matching reserve fund is maintained by the insurance carrier, it is routinely monitored and audited by government regulatory agencies.

Contrary to common belief, there are no fees in a fixed-annuity
contract. If you have ever read about annual administration fees or
other charges related to annuities, you were probably reading about
variable annuities, not fixed-indexed annuities. (Because this book does
not deal with variable annuities, and I do not endorse them, I cannot
recommend or advise against the purchase of such instruments.)

As for fixed-indexed annuities, there are no hidden fees other than,
in the scenario described previously, the 2.5 percent the company receives as a share of earnings from bond investments made from accumulated deposits of client principal. And that 2.5 percent is probably
the source of most reports of fixed-annuity annual "fees" of 2 percent
or more. That's fair enough, but the more appropriate term would be
"shared earnings" from bonds purchased by the insurance carrier.

So why not take your own $100,000 principal, buy the same
bonds, and keep the whole 6 percent gain for yourself? If you are
a skilled, knowledgeable investor who can find a relatively risk-free
bond, avoid all the fees incurred by using other investment advisors,
and be reasonably assured that your original principal will be safely
guaranteed against future bond default and other factors, please do!
Remember that while annuity carriers do take a cut (in this case 2.5
percent) for company overhead, government-mandated documentation, client notices, agent commissions, and company profits (most
agents are independent contractors, not company employees), your
$100,000 will be guaranteed by the government-mandated reserve
fund, no matter what happens. You will share in the earnings based
on carrier bond purchases, and your portion of the earnings will accumulate on a tax-deferred basis (so many people underestimate the
value of deferral). With most fixed annuities, you will also receive a
lifetime of income distributions, meaning distributions will continue
after the ten-year payout period following the annuity's maturation.

So that's the trade-off. There's no free lunch, of course, but you
can see the advantages of nesting a portion of your portfolio outside
typical market-risk scenarios. Of course, insurance carriers might
profit if you choose to cash out early. On the other hand, they as-

sume risk to buy the bonds in order to allow you to earn yearly tax-deferred income. When you choose to cash out early, the carrier's risk exposure in the bond market increases according to the amount you withdraw before the annuity's maturation. So a fair and equitable surrender charge offsets the carrier's risk. I've said more than once in this book that some companies go overboard with their surrender charges, greedily larding their own coffers with additional profit well beyond the risk mitigation of your early withdrawal, but most are fair and equitable.

Meanwhile, remember that most annuities offer a 10 percent penalty-free withdrawal every year, and the best advice I can give when gauging whether or not to purchase an annuity is to take a hard look at that 10 percent. Assume the worst: that you will need to make a 10 percent withdrawal every year. Would that be enough to cover your basic living expenses, along with your other savings and guaranteed income sources? Maybe you should have a good stash of additional liquid cash reserves for emergencies, another annuity, a life-insurance policy with medical riders, and a bank CD or two—all outside of any risk-based scenario in the market. All told, when you're purchasing annuities, you should look at the long-term advantages alongside the potential downside, and plan to avoid early withdrawal literally at all cost. In short, every phase of financial planning should be taken seriously and studied carefully in terms of your current living expenses, projected future expenses in retirement, and any anticipated long-term expense increases (of home utility costs, property taxes, etc.) based on inflation or other factors.

Some clients ask, "Do agents profit from surrender charges?" Let me answer in three words: Not at all. In fact, insurance companies have chargeback schedules that go along with commission payments. Chargeback schedules allow insurance carriers to recapture portions of an agent's commission if a client opts out or surrenders the annuity contract early on.

Here's an example of one annuity's chargeback schedule if a client surrenders during the first year of the annuity contract. If the client surrenders during the first four months of the first year, the agent must return 100 percent of his commission. If the client surrenders between months five and eight of the first year, the agent must return

66.67 percent of his commission. If the client surrenders between months nine and twelve, the agent must return 33.33 percent of his commission.

Another annuity requires a 100 percent commission chargeback if the agent's client surrenders at any time during the entire first year of the contract. If a client surrenders this particular annuity during the second year, agents are required to give back 50 percent of commissions paid to that point.

Imagine how trying this can be—especially for newer agents who are just getting started in the business. That's why I always teach (and frankly implore) every new agent to provide complete product disclosure to potential clients, along with an exhaustive process of discovery to assess the client's real needs. Obviously, it is in both the client's and the annuity salesperson's best interest to avoid early surrender.

Many commissions are paid up-front after the annuity contract is approved and issued to the purchaser. To ease the pain of contract surrender, some carriers offer "trail commissions" to agents, which are paid out according to a schedule over a period of time. But nothing can replace thorough analysis and disclosure *first* to ensure that the client buys the right annuity for her and *second* to help safeguard the agent's commission.

Here's a hypothetical example of an agent's commission payout. A typical contract offers the agent a 4 to 7 percent commission for a ten-year contract with a 5 percent **immediate premium bonus** going to the purchaser. (Remember, commissions vary dramatically from company to company and can also change depending on the overall length of the contract and the size of any commission bonus attached.) If a client purchased a $100,000 contract of this type, the agent would receive a commission check for $7,000 for the first-year premium and the client's starting account value would be $105,000. Annuities for shorter durations, which are called MYGAs (see page 25), offer commissions as low as 0.75 percent. In general, commissions grow according to the duration of the annuity, meaning less commission for a lesser term of maturity, which may explain certain agents' enthusiasm for offering some annuities in very age-inappropriate situations.

Standard annuity commissions have never been out of line with those in other industries, such as real estate. While real-estate sales commissions in some states cannot be set in stone by law, any homeowner knows (or soon discovers) that residential real-estate commissions typically vary from 4 to 7 percent—or more, given market conditions, the condition and location of a house, agent concessions, agent marketing costs, and other factors.

Few people realize that real-estate agents may see commissions of 10 percent or more for sales of raw land, commercial/retail, and industrial properties. This is often because the latter involve limited inventory, remote locations, greater marketing costs, and highly specialized expertise. As a result, higher commissions are required to attract qualified personnel with enough personal capital to market and sell a property.

Since most annuities are highly complex instruments, requiring an extensive presentation process and agent training period, annuities offer higher commissions than those in some other industries. For example, some fixed-annuity contracts contain as many as 120 pages of text describing allowable contract options during and after the term. A typical residential real-estate contract might include twenty pages, more or less, of contract terminology to present to clients, thus requiring less time and technical explanation.

Certain automakers have offered commissions as high as 15 percent for various makes and models; of course, these commissions are shared by the salesperson, the sales and marketing staff, and the dealership itself. Ask anyone in the car business if auto sales are a walk in the park. No way! Car sales are complicated by intense competition, the economy, inventory problems—you name it.

Sales commissions in the securities industry are even more variable and can be more complex to track, but it is not unusual to find a financial planner who charges each of her clients a continuous annual percentage fee based on the total value of the client's entire investment portfolio. This means that a planner who charged a 1 to 3 percent fee per year for a portfolio valued at $1 million would receive commissions of $10,000 to $30,000 a year for each client she represented. Do the math to compute the earnings of a financial planner with a client base of anywhere from 30 to 300 clients.

Yet financial planners operate in a variety of different ways. Some do business on a fee-only basis. Others make money on commissions paid through the sales of securities, which are generated whenever they recommend changes in a client's portfolio. One fact is self-evident: none of these people work for free. Why should they? Expertise and experience is hard won, as is the often grinding effort to stay in the game.

The challenge for every consumer is to find a representative who makes decisions based on the welfare of the consumer instead of his own commissions. Finding such a professional, you know by now, is not necessarily a walk in the park. Many of us consider anything above 10 percent to be an **excessive commission**. Certain annuity contracts include longer contract maturity periods, which leave a larger budget for higher commissions, along with higher fixed rates for the consumer and a greater bonus potential.

I can't stress enough the importance of thorough contract review. To most effectively meet your own needs, you must compare products and their features. Weigh the limitations against the benefits, because you won't find the commissions mentioned anywhere in the typical annuity contract or brochure. It's up to you to look for the highest number of consumer-friendly features.

If clients accept my strategies and purchase annuities or life policies through me, I receive a commission from the issuing company for the purchase of those products. Every one of my clients knows this basic fact from the beginning. Really, the most important piece of information for my clients to know is that I am not paid out of their principal. I do not favor any particular line of products, nor am I bound by any company to represent its product line. I am independent, and I do not charge fees for overall financial planning. I also choose to be licensed to provide an array of recommendations beyond annuities, which gives me enhanced abilities to guide clients as they prepare for retirement, in addition to helping clients who are already in retirement.

Expect the same standards from the planner you choose.

CHAPTER 11

Long-Term Care, Social Security, Taxes ... and Other Things that May Drive Us Crazy Before We Die

I BELIEVE PEOPLE CAN MEET THEIR RETIREMENT GOALS BY USING a combination of products offered by the best providers in the insurance industry. I call this approach safe-retirement planning. Safe-retirement planning is streamlined and efficient, and it works. The ultimate goal is to give that streamlined efficiency to a client so he can feel comfortable, and that comfort comes from being able to comprehend the substance of a retirement plan inside and out. Some people may be comfortable with an element of risk in their portfolios, but others come to a point where risk is unacceptable. A great many planners develop complex strategies that leave clients unaware of the actual risk level they've accepted.

I recently met a potential client with an asset base that was heavily leveraged in securities. As I got to know him, I was amazed to discover just how uncomfortable he was about the position he was in. He'd been placed in that situation through intimidation—someone had told him to accept such risk without question, and that he had no alternative other than risk. So the fellow, who eventually did become my client, was into risk exposure up to his neck, all the while unaware of just how severe his risk level was. Every client *must* thoroughly understand the instruments she invests in, or she should not invest in them. The educational process can be painstaking and very time-consuming, which is why so many planners instead lead their clients into a deep, dark forest called "trust me."

"Trust me," they say. "I know what I'm doing. Let me do my job, and you do yours." The ability to teach is a gift, and some planners lack this gift. They'll tell you it's their way or the highway. With this type of planner, you will find yourself with many more questions than answers.

Other planners work hard to provide a level of education. They strive to help their clients understand where their money is going, which really helps in the long run. After leaving their planner's office, most clients forget the details of a) their own financial plan and b) what needs to be done to properly monitor and manage the plan. In most cases, after clients are educated, the strategy should be simplified enough to allow them to manage the plan on their own, if they so choose.

Long-Term Care Needs

By now, you know that I think traditional LTC insurance is not right for most of my clients because it is often far too expensive, and some cannot qualify. By now, you also know that with annuities, you can plan for long-term care, no matter what health or money issues you have.

I keep getting back to LTC insurance because, for me, it's a metaphor for many of the misunderstandings that are so commonplace in today's financial services industry. We are all told to get LTC insurance, and that such coverage is the only way to protect our lifestyles. Yet no one tells us what to do if we cannot afford such insurance, or if we don't qualify for health reasons. LTC insurance companies are not at all sure whether the rates they charge will provide enough assets to cover their future exposure or the benefits they promise. On top of that, health insurance laws could change dramatically, which may affect LTC coverage requirements, which in turn may drive a shift in premiums.

Most people I meet who have an LTC policy think they understand it, but they don't. They think they have lifetime coverage, but in fact, they do not. They lack a real understanding of LTC policy elimination periods, they don't know how to trigger their coverage, and the LTC product itself is something akin to a "learn-by-doing" process for insurers—they're learning by doing, but at your expense. I don't like it.

Putting even more pressure on the credibility of the LTC policy is the rising cost of Medigap insurance, which is squeezing more health care dollars out of our pockets than ever before. But we still have to plan more effectively for health care costs, so I always advise my clients about long-term health planning, especially on behalf of a surviving spouse.

Meanwhile, our current national health care system is in crisis, so where should you go for future assurance of quality long-term medical care? Instead of pouring thousands of dollars a year into an unproven insurance policy, why not go the asset-based insurance route?

Asset-based LTC means adding an LTC provision to an annuity or life-insurance policy. If you are considering the purchase of an annuity or life-insurance policy with an LTC rider, be aware that while this method may be more cost effective, it may not provide the full coverage of traditional LTC insurance. On the other hand, if you buy a traditional LTC policy now, it may not be what you actually need in the future. For example, what if you purchase a costly LTC policy today, only to discover an alternative product twenty years from now? Imagine if a national universal health care plan were adopted, and you'd already paid $30,000 in premiums for an antiquated LTC policy. Do you think the insurance company would feel sorry for you and give you your money back?

Those who've already purchased an LTC policy probably did so when they were younger, so their premiums aren't as steep. I might advise them to keep the policy, depending on just how high those premiums are. But if you are sixty-five or older with a $50,000 income, you will pay $3,000 to $4,000 a year for LTC insurance—close to 10 percent of your income. I consider that a very expensive health care alternative.

Consider this example: an elderly woman who had LTC insurance for ten years went into the hospital and died the next day. Her expensive LTC insurance premiums were all for nothing. Sure, she had protection all those years, but she never received more than a day's benefit. No wonder people are angry about LTC policies.

Social Security and Taxes

What makes me really angry is taxation of our Social Security benefits. People pay taxes on a tax when they're taxed on their Social Security benefits. While you are working, Social Security taxes are withheld from your paychecks. Once you start receiving the money you paid into Social Security, you're taxed all over again! When is it payback time for the average taxpayer?

Many annuity salespeople tout the tax-deferred advantage of annuities over other forms of saving and investment. You'll probably hear it mentioned several times during an annuity sales presentation. But some salespeople may fail to fully explain how tax deferral works, simply because they lack comprehensive knowledge of the subject themselves.

To take the guesswork out of this important aspect of the fixed annuity, let's set aside complex mathematical tables and get to the heart of it. First, when the annuity matures, the annuity owner will get a tax bill from the IRS after years of tax-deferred earnings. For now, let's put the tax bill in the context of a conventional mortgage payment, or the two basic parts of a mortgage payment: principal and interest.

When you choose to annuitize your policy and begin receiving monthly payments, or distributions, the government will consider part of each payment a nontaxable repayment of the principal you originally put into the annuity. The other portion of your monthly distribution will be based on interest earnings you accumulated, tax deferred, over the growth cycle of the annuity. The IRS will tax those earnings, based on the tax-deferred earnings portion of each monthly payment you receive. Yet the equation is more complex than that, and surprisingly, that's to your advantage. The government computes what it calls an "exclusion ratio" into your required tax payment, which is calculated by dividing your initial principal contribution to the annuity contract by the total amount of payouts you would expect to receive during the entire payout period.

Here's a theoretical example, without the vital input of your tax professional, of course: let's look at a typical annuity that begins with a $100,000 initial contribution from the annuity owner. After a few years have passed, the owner is sixty-five and ready to receive distributions of $800 a month. Let's say IRS life-expectancy calculations determine that a sixty-five-year-old annuity owner would receive those payments for nineteen and a half years. The total value of your annuity contract would therefore be worth $800 × 12 months a year × 19.5 years, or $187,200.

In this scenario, the IRS applies a 53.4 percent exclusion ratio to the total value of the annuity payout of $187,200, which is nearly twice the original $100,000 contribution of principal. The IRS essentially excludes the original $100,000 from taxation, and taxes the remainder, or $87,200. In real numbers, the sixty-five-year-old annuity owner will pay no tax at all on 53.4 percent of $9,600 a year ($800 a month × 12 = $9,600), which amounts to $5,126 in tax-free annual payments. The remaining amount of the distributions, $4,474, would be taxed according to the owner's income category and other considerations.

That's the basic scenario, although other options involve a more complex process involving the transfer of funds from one tax-deferred vehicle to another, thus compounding earnings for extended periods of time until the owner finally decides to receive income. But all these tactics, and the preceding hypothetical example, are subject to various rules and should be carefully and routinely reviewed by a qualified tax expert. Because IRS and state rules and regulations are a moving target, always seek the qualified advice of an experienced tax attorney and/or a CPA. You will find additional details about the basics of exclusion ratios and other matters in IRS Publication 939, *General Rule for Pensions and Annuities* (http://www.irs.gov/pub/irs-pdf/p939.pdf).

If you withdraw money from an annuity, which may or may not trigger a surrender charge, you would also pay ordinary income taxes on the withdrawal. The IRS may impose an additional 10 percent penalty on that withdrawal if you are under the age of fifty-nine and a half.

You may or may not hear about some or all of the above in a sales presentation, nor would you find such equations in certain annuity contracts. Much of this is up to you to learn. Consider the sample equations as a starting point, knowing that every situation takes a different turn, and myriad possibilities exist that may be to your advantage as an annuitant. That's why you need the additional expertise of qualified professionals both before and during the annuity payout period.

The same applies to other missing numbers. In some fixed-indexed annuity contracts, for example, no actual short- or long-term rate of return might be mentioned. The contract probably won't suggest how your fixed-indexed annuity might perform over the full accumulation cycle either. Other than a few general statements regarding minimum guarantees, annual fixed or "declaration" rates, and other data regarding deposit allocations, most tax equations and other pertinent information will probably not be there. Thus, be prepared to have a qualified expert—someone outside the annuity sales process—ready to delve into the fine print. This is your right, and moreover, it's an obligation to yourself. You must enter into any annuity contract with your eyes wide open, with all pertinent facts and figures in front of you from day one.

Leaving It Up to the Broker

Another notorious retirement income drain comes from leaving all of your financial decisions to a broker—especially a busy one who works for a big company. If you're in this situation, don't be surprised if nothing changes during a short- or long-term market decline. Should the broker be making some moves on your behalf? Yes, no, or maybe. Maybe she thinks the market will come around again and resolve the loss. "Maybe the turnaround will come," she'll say, pointing to the long-term ten-year cycle of commitment you need to give her in order to realize recovery of your loss.

Maybe it's your fault for failing to step in and make the broker do something. After all, it is your money. You should be watching your own money with far greater interest than your broker—who may in fact have little interest at all. After all, she may have hundreds of other clients to worry about, so speak up! You can do one of three things. You can step in and make lots of noise to make your broker work for you. You can leave your broker altogether and find one who is willing to work for you. You can do nothing and stay with the program, but how much can you afford to lose?

I recently had a client who had some of his portfolio with me and some with a major brokerage company. After twenty-five years with the brokerage company, he came to the realization that although he'd repeatedly asked his rep to adjust his asset allocation to provide more income, nothing had ever happened. His broker never listened and never made changes. The allocation remained the same, as if the client had never made a single request. He decided to pull his brokerage assets and give them to me to manage, but before he did, he called his broker of twenty-five years to politely say goodbye. The rep was on another line when he was told that the client was moving everything out of his portfolio, but the rep did have his secretary relay two words to my new client: "Good luck."

From that day on, we established the client's first comprehensive financial plan. He'd had no such thing before. Was this the fault of the brokerage firm? No, it was the fault of the broker, and the client, for failing to demand a comprehensible, comprehensive retirement plan. What signals the lack of such a plan?

For one, I've been able to sit down with many new clients, look over their financial plans, and find a common glaring omission: the lack of **springing power of attorney**, which is power of attorney that only comes into play if the person in question becomes incapacitated. Without this one basic planning tool, you may be leaving vital decisions up to the discretion of the state. Seek the advice of an attorney who specializes in law related to the elderly to make sure your power of attorney is properly drawn up. Also, keep in mind that one type of power of attorney covers health issues, and the other covers financial matters. An attorney specializing in elder law will help you determine the right kind of power of attorney for your situation.

Sometimes clients place the blame on a broker when actually the client is entirely to blame. People tend to get mad when they start losing money. When they're making money, they couldn't care less how their assets are allocated or what condition their portfolio may be in. Over the course of a year, changes are sometimes made based on a broker's recommendations—changes clients may not understand. But if they trust their brokers, they'll probably approve the change.

Sometimes I have to explain to clients what a broker has done with their assets. In those cases, I don't blame the broker, because it is the responsibility of the clients themselves to understand changes made to their portfolios. In order to keep from going broke in retirement, you must accept the fact that you are the bottom line. You need to effectively track your own portfolio, which may take time and may require a bit of extra reading. If your broker or financial planner lacks the time to help you understand what you have, it's time to find someone else or go it alone.

When this kind of misunderstanding winds up at my desk, the new client and I go back and try to rebuild some understanding of the broker's market moves. I keep things simple and make sure the client understands what has been done. Then, together, the client and I go through a lot of one-on-one reviews. Some people are afraid to ask for this kind of attention, but they deserve it. Clients should expect this type of service from their financial planner, and if their planner is unable to provide it, they should look for someone who can.

CHAPTER 12

The Financial World ... According to Reindel

L ET'S SUMMARIZE THE REAL-WORLD BASICS YOU'VE LEARNED SO
far about financial survival in retirement:

- The government and corporations are dumping the burden
  of retirement income on you and future generations.
- Believe what you want about government plans for Social
  Security, but the system is completely broken and may be
  well beyond repair.
- Corporations once provided jobs for life. They also provided
  dignified retirements through well-funded retirement programs. Unfortunately, that's no longer true.
- Corporations are rapidly phasing out defined-benefit pensions in favor of cash-balance plans.
- The use of individual employee 401(k) programs has led to
  the move away from pension plans and Social Security.
- From the baby-boom generation on, retirees will be on their
  own. Recent political and corporate changes make that very
  clear.
- Wherever you currently work, corporate and government
  financial planning is very limited. Your financial retirement
  strategy will be entirely up to you. Be ready for it.

When government and corporate planners developed models to
fund their liabilities in the past, did they ever for a minute consider
basing their plans on stock-market returns? Of course not! They were

required by law to guarantee their income projections for every retiree, and those projections were based on the most conservative financial principles available.

When the government considered "privatizing" Social Security,
encouraging stock market investments with private funds, people
went crazy. But I predict that those who promoted such a preposter-
ous notion have yet to suffer the full political consequences of their
actions. That's because most people in this country yearn for conservative planning, which has always formed the solid foundation of
retirement dreams. And any financial planner who fails to grasp this
simple concept is headed for trouble. In fact, I suggest that she look
into another line of work.

I feel equally passionate about the long-term care issue. I do not
own LTC insurance because our health care system is flawed and
in need of repair. When I poll audiences at my seminars, I generally find that few have purchased LTC insurance. Why? Because it's
expensive, and few consumers understand how it works. So is it fair
that those who can afford insurance do not have to spend down their
assets immediately, while others who cannot afford insurance or are
in poor health are required by law—and a load of convoluted rules—
to spend what they worked a lifetime to save? In some cases, the latter have been forced to sell their homes, thus jeopardizing the future
comfort and security of their spouses.

Again, this is where planning comes in. We can help mitigate
some of the problem, but the government needs to do more to help
people obtain affordable long-term health care. We hope the government will take the helm, and state and federal governments and
the health care industry are hoping that the middle class—that's *us*,
by the way—will somehow figure out how to handle the problem
on our own. Nonsense! Ever try to battle outrageous hospital bills
and/or pharmaceutical costs—costs that would have been considered
criminal in a bygone era? This type of responsibility is beyond our
control, and so it goes with LTC.

If you are young and healthy and have considerable financial
means, you can buy LTC insurance. But what about Mrs. Smith,
an elderly woman living on a fixed income? Or Mr. Jones, who was

recently diagnosed with a chronic illness? How fair is this kind of system to them? How fair is it that senior citizens must be impoverished in order to receive Medicaid benefits?

I do believe in the positive development of a citizen-equitable health care system in this country. Why? Because the largest mass of Americans ever born are about to enter their retirement years. I believe the people will drive the vote, which will foster a new generation of politicians who will enact an effective health care reform plan. Until then, we are in crisis, a health care crisis destined to explode before frightened politicians move to fix the system.

In the meantime, annuities can be powerful tools for Medicaid planning. Why shouldn't you use annuities, when the government allows you to guarantee your money through annuities and other insurance products? Why should anyone over sixty-five put any money at risk? It makes me crazy to know that although Medicaid planning laws in most states allow us to preserve our assets through annuities and other instruments, most people seem reluctant to act on this information, as if they may be doing something wrong.

Yes, you'll need the professional guidance of an attorney specializing in elder law to follow the rules to a "T," but insurance-based Medicaid planning is done every day. If you fail to make your plan, you'll be stuck with the government's plan for you—and you might not like it. Even though you've paid for Medicaid with your hard-earned tax dollars, you can't use it unless you spend all of your assets! How absurdly unfair is that? That's exactly why measures have been written into individual state Medicaid regulations. Those provisions are there for people and their professional advisors to preserve retirement assets. While Medicaid planning is just as critical as tax planning, I still hear people say it's unfair to take advantage of the government to use such provisions—which were in fact given to us *by the government!* Would you ever say, "Gee, the government is hurting this year, so I think I'll donate this year's interest deduction on the house to the IRS"?

You have the same right to Medicaid planning as you do to your home-interest deduction. Of course, if you have lots of money and good health, you can have the best of all worlds, with some LTC insurance and other Medicaid planning tools. Once your LTC insurance is used up, you'll be back to square one, and your other instruments will kick in.

Certain states offer an option called the Partnership Program. With this program, you can buy $200,000 worth of insurance to shield $200,000 in assets. This sounds okay at first glance, but is it really fair? I think not. Only a person with good health and enough assets can participate, but what about ailing Mrs. Smith, who can't buy insurance for health and/or financial reasons? Because she lives in a state that offers the Partnership Program, the state has no obligation to maintain an assigned risk pool, so she's out of luck. Mrs. Smith can't qualify for LTC insurance, either, so she's facing a dilemma. Even though she currently has $200,000 in assets, she must spend all of her money—all the way down to $1,600, in fact, in her state—before Medicaid will kick in to pay for her nursing-home care.

Is this a fair system? No, it isn't. Is this the way it is? Yes, it is, and most people don't understand how the system works. Most people simply accept the fact that they will be forced into poverty if they get sick. And that is one *sick* way for state and federal governments to treat people.

Where Annuities Come In

Fixed-indexed annuities are great retirement savings tools. Please write that down: fixed-indexed annuities. Some fixed-indexed annuities also have features that may help provide for long-term health care if one cannot afford or obtain traditional LTC insurance. I think much of the controversy about fixed-indexed annuities can be assigned to one thing: denial.

Countless advisors who shunned the fixed-indexed annuity and other conservative instruments lost heavily in risk investments. They screwed up. Period. And how do some of them deal with it? They refuse to admit they were wrong, that's how. They continue to trumpet the same investment philosophies that got them in trouble in the first place. The truth is that annuities would have given their clients a stable, fail-safe platform for preserving their retirement lifestyles.

Did I say that every single fixed-indexed annuity is perfect? No way. Did I say that you should never take on risk with a security? Of course not. Some people enjoy taking a bit of risk. Have you been to a casino lately? Look across a room filled with slot machines and count the number of seniors. Some seniors like to gamble, but the wise ones do it with a solid, guaranteed income stream at home. They might take a little mad money to Atlantic City or Las Vegas, but they know how to budget for loss. Gambling equals loss, eventually. The smart ones know that.

When things are going well at the slot machines, people like to brag and celebrate. When things are going well on Wall Street, risk-takers love to chide conservative savers. But when things go awry, when the risk-takers are afraid, they clam up, because they don't like to talk about their fears. And people are afraid. I have clients with $1 million in assets who are afraid of running out of money in retirement. I can see it in their eyes, even if they don't come right out and say it. Those who have made mistakes in the past are particularly reluctant to admit it.

I will tell every man and woman reading this book what we've heard all our lives: everyone makes mistakes, and the financial arena can be very complex. Even an absolute financial genius makes a wrongheaded call from time to time, so the above-average Joe is in for a challenge. I want to reach out to everyone who took a hit in the post-9/11 and post-2008 marketplace and say, "Fear not. Study your mistakes. You are in some very good company in that regard. Ninety percent of the American investment community took some kind of hit. Now, we have history behind us and a wealth of safe-haven opportunity ahead." Take advantage of that opportunity while you can.

We don't want to dwell upon our innermost fears: the federal deficit, our horrible health care system, the trade deficit, the disappearing Social Security coffers, and so on. We hate to talk about uncertainty in general, but we hate talking about running out of money even more. Yet more than once a month, I say to a client: "Keep doing what you are doing, and you will go broke before you die."

Nobody wants to hear that, especially those with a **confirmation bias**, a phenomenon wherein we focus on information that confirms previously held beliefs and ignore information that contradicts those beliefs. No one wants to believe that we've been dumped into shark-infested financial waters by our government and big corporations, the same entities that used to manage our retirement funds. While we have yet to feel the brunt of this kind of institutional irresponsibility, it will eventually affect the national economy in untold ways, and at a horrendous cost.

My job is to guide you through the process and let you see the results for yourself. And when you do, I think you will accept my recommendations. Do you have this kind of relationship with your current broker or financial planner? If not, why not? Would your current planner consider such a request an outrageous challenge of his professional authority? If so, you should be outraged enough to change planners. Proceed to the next chapter, and I'll give you other outrageous things to think about.

CHAPTER 13

Outrageous Truths and Myths Exposed

Long-Term Care

One easy way to lose money is to buy a "pioneering" version of LTC insurance. I use the term "pioneering" because LTC coverage is still in a formative period. By necessity, the LTC insurance system will undergo a lot of repair during the next twenty years. First of all, most people who need LTC insurance can't afford it—at least not without stripping away their retirement funds. The price of LTC insurance is simply outrageous.

State and federal governments have a vested interest in leaving consumers to sort things out with LTC insurance. If they don't deal with it, the rest of us are left—once again—to manage our own destinies in a financial jungle of health care insurance providers. My advice is to be careful when considering LTC coverage for now; instead, check all the options that are available, such as asset-based LTC. If you are a veteran, check out the options available to you through the Veterans' Administration.

At the same time, let your regional politicians know that we need better health care guarantees for our tax dollars, and that we have a terrible health care system in need of reform. We still pay too much for health insurance. The majority of us still have to pay down retirement assets to poverty level for LTC, and we still can't use our tax dollars to buy our own health insurance. We can still have all the government-subsidized health care we want for nothing, but only if we have nothing.

Yet there is an answer to all this via safe-retirement planning tools. If you're young, advisors might tell you to buy LTC coverage and pay for it for forty years, in the highly unlikely case that you might need it. My advice to the young and old: be careful and carefully think through these decisions before you make them. In the meantime, those millions of us who are beyond the ability to effectively afford LTC coverage will have to take to the streets and demand change—or we'll plan right now for our own LTC with a combination of safe-retirement strategies.

Some of those strategies include various forms of life insurance, which can have riders attached to provide some aspects of LTC. Fixed annuities can also provide a solution. In any event, you need the counsel of someone familiar with every rule in the book regarding taxes, Medicare, and Medicaid laws and myriad other factors to make good decisions. Make no mistake—LTC is a complex topic that requires more than just the hasty purchase of a typical LTC policy.

Younger boomers caring for elderly parents may not know what the Deficit Reduction Act did to subsidized LTC, but they will see the effects. Here's what happened: to reduce the deficit, the federal government sought to gain $39 billion by changing the Medicaid "look-back" period from three to five years. That means the government now looks back five years into an applicant's financial history to find asset giveaways to adult children and other heirs. Five years. If, during that period, you gifted money to spend down toward Medicaid qualification, your waiting period for application acceptance may be extended accordingly. Some planners may not be aware of the extended look-back period. As always, check the regulations in your own area. If you or a loved one are in this situation now, I strongly urge you to consult an elder-law attorney who specializes in your local Medicaid regulations.

I know of one couple who spent thousands with various "professional care managers," all of whom promised to help the couple put the wife's mother in a Medicaid-sponsored nursing home. More than eighteen months later, and after wasting thousands upon thousands of dollars on consulting and nursing-home fees, the wife's mother was still waiting to become a Medicaid applicant. Then, an elder-law attorney stepped in, and things began to happen.

Medicaid is more than an institution. It is a tortuous maze of rules, all of which seem to change according to location. The rules are administered by people in your state and county, so it is imperative that the elder-law attorney you consult has a good deal of familiarity with the state/local system.

Spousal Refusal

Check your own state's Medicaid regulations, but in some states, you might be able to protect your assets from the perils of LTC with an option called "spousal refusal." However, this method is very state-specific, and in some extreme cases, attorneys have advised their clients to divorce instead. Again, please consult an elder-law attorney when considering such matters.

Are You Really Sacrificing Gains?

While I would applaud Congress for making it unlawful for any-one over sixty-five to have 401(k)s, IRAs, or other money or assets at risk, that's not likely to happen. I suggest that you can enact a similar rule for your own use. Call it your very own Rule of Common Sense against Risk: you would voluntarily prohibit yourself from keeping your assets at risk after age sixty-five. No financial advisor, government official, federal law, friend, or family member has the power to dictate otherwise.

When you buy an annuity, you refuse risk and pass it on to the insurance company. You also forfeit the possibility of receiving, say, 12 percent returns and agree to accept 6 to 7 percent returns. But in the summer of 2007, short-term gains neared 14 to 18 percent on the Dow and S&P—just before the ensuing crash. Later, everyone saw the real truth in the ten-year spread, where the long-term gains were revealed: 5.1 percent for the S&P and 5.6 percent for the Dow.

People with annuities did better than that. Much better. On top of that, they had planned their household budgets to live within their guaranteed incomes. They escaped the pain and suffering of market angst. Were you one of those people? If not, you can start right now and be ready for the next big market crash or major recession. Start by looking at the variety of modern fixed annuities in today's marketplace. There are other tools for safe-retirement planning, of course, but annuities are a good place to start, and some of the newer annuities have more consumer-friendly surrender charges, more flexible surrender periods, income bonuses, and other features—all while allowing you to keep some of your assets in the market to capture gains. With fixed annuities, those very gains will be preserved forever.

Making Equities Dealers Responsible for Their Actions

Most people meanwhile have no idea of how much risk they are taking until it's too late. They have no real concept of the way world events, both major and miniscule, affect their own holdings close to home. For most of us, risk is a meaningless word until we feel the loss. I've had friends who suffered devastating losses during the last crash. They said it felt like the sickening up and down lurch of a roller coaster, one in which you find yourself flat broke when you climb out at the end of the ride.

One of my clients put it best: "Sure, there's risk, but you pay your money to take the ride. That's because you don't believe there is any risk at the time." That's a cardinal sin of financial planning. His planner never told him about the risk—he only talked about the wonderful potential for rewards. Instead, he'd been assured of having "a safety harness" and "brakes on the roller-coaster car." But his planner forgot to mention that the car would be attached to other cars containing other investors just like him, and that the brakes would be controlled by someone else: that is, the financial planner himself, who was waiting to greet them all with bad news at the bottom of the last hill.

This client told me, "You don't really think about the risk until you're hurtling through space." I suggest that you start thinking about the roller coaster right now, especially if you are over sixty-five. Are you hurtling through space on the fast track, or are you ready to consider enacting your personal Rule of Common Sense against Risk?

It's up to you, but meanwhile, let's examine some common misconceptions. First, many people erroneously think that a bond portfolio has no risk. Of course you have risk in a bond portfolio! If you pay $100 for a bond and interest rates go up, the bond value goes down accordingly. You lose money if you need to cash out when interest rates are high. That's risk, and people sixty-five or older have no business taking that kind of risk. Moreover, their IRA and 401(k) retirement funds should no longer be in stock- and bond-market assets, period. If you are over sixty-five and in this situation, I think you should get out of risk now and get into safe-retirement planning.

These days, it is perfectly legal—and sometimes encouraged by the equity industry—to use IRAs as trading accounts. Even 401(k)s are used to move assets in and out of mutual funds, and many people who exercise that option have no idea what they are doing. They are the same people who might act on a hot stock tip from some TV guru, or blindly follow the advice of a charismatic neighbor—right into the poorhouse. If you are one of these risk-prone individuals, consider your age and the appropriate amount of risk you should be taking, and if you're over sixty-five, find a genuine safe-retirement advocate and safeguard some measure of guaranteed income. We're in for a wild roller-coaster ride in the coming years and, for many of us, it's time to get off.

The documentation supplied for company-sponsored 401(k) plans offer either the most simplistic (and thus inadequate) or the most complex explanations possible. The former fail to inform and the latter confound you with high-level terminology. In general, company guidelines keep the truth beyond the grasp of most people.

Anyone over fifty should be required to sign an affidavit of acknowledgment to verify that they thoroughly comprehend the market-based assets they are about to commit to potential catastrophic and irretrievable loss, especially when they are shifting assets into or out of their IRAs and 401(k)s. Actually, measures are in the works in some states to require planners to have their clients sign such affidavits. If you are considering purchasing equities and are not presented with such an affidavit, ask if an affidavit is required by that particular company or provider.

In the absence of law, investors should be required to acknowledge in writing the potential jeopardy of their paper investments. In

the near future, some states may require such a written acknowledgment to be digitally signed each and every time an investor autho-
rizes a trade. Like the warning label on a pack of cigarettes, such
acknowledgments will give investors a moment of reflection before
moving forward. I'm all for them, because they make both the client
and the advisor work harder to clarify every detail of an investment.

What I'm getting at is the real need for you to demand complete,
detailed answers to every question you may have, no matter how
long it takes, and to demand these answers according to your schedule. Some people in my business are actually trained to make consumers feel uneasy about asking the same questions more than once
or twice. You have the right to ask the same question five times—a
dozen times, if you like—until the answer becomes crystal clear to
you. After all, it's your money at stake, not theirs.

The Importance of Buy-In from Both Spouses

In most states, the signatures of both spouses are required before a jointly owned home can be sold. Why not require something
similar for jointly owned retirement accounts, especially when those
accounts are probably worth more than the jointly owned home?
But due to the topsy-turvy pretzel logic governing retirement assets,
few such measures have been enacted or enforced to cover securities trades and annuity sales, so beware. While many states currently
lack such measures, you and your significant other can make a pact
stating that neither of you would make trades or other retirement
acquisitions without written permission from the other spouse.

If required by law, this type of affidavit would bring a dramatic
and healthy upheaval to the equities industry, because women are
far more cautious about risk than men. Husbands are far more apt
to jump into active trading with jointly held accounts. I have seen
first-hand the look of surprise on a wife's face when she discovers
her husband's trading antics. So many wives have no idea what their
husbands are up to with jointly held funds, but wives are statistically
more likely to survive their husbands in retirement. This pact would
at least get both spouses started on the road to sound retirement
planning together. Husbands, if you consider this to be an imposi

tion, consider your better half to be your best excuse to step back from a pending investment. Take a closer look with the one person in the world who stands to gain or lose along with you.

Here's yet another reality. Another tragedy occurs after a spouse with a full pension is gone. In most cases, the surviving spouse winds up with only a partial pension. After the pensioner dies, the survivor has an income problem. In these cases, I have to act quickly to bring the survivor up to an acceptable level of income.

I encourage clients to choose plans that allow for the establishment of enhanced income for a surviving spouse after the primary pension recipient passes away. Will such policies and strategies ever be implemented industry-wide? Maybe, and maybe not. All I can say is that we're working on it; meanwhile, I've shown you some things you can do to get ahead of the curve.

Timing *Is* Everything

Again, I am not entirely opposed to risk or equity investment. If someone has $85,000 worth of guaranteed income per year from pensions, Social Security, and other sources, she can afford risk. However, people who can count on income like that in retirement are few and far between. Most of the people I work with have no business delving into active trading, speculative high-risk equities, or any other form of investment risk.

I'll give you one such example. I recently met with an extremely astute businessman who had an uncanny knack for market prognosis. His wife was heavily invested in real estate, and he wanted to get her out. He knew the mortgage crisis was coming, and he knew it was time to look for alternatives. But she was so deeply obsessed with her real-estate holdings that he had to devise a scheme to convince her to divest. To do it, he treated her to an offer she couldn't refuse—a thrilling 100-day cruise around the globe. He hoped she would escape from real estate long enough to see a better life.

Their cruise was scheduled for January 2000. Before they left, he told her he was temporarily cashing out of the market and putting his $3 million in assets into a money-market fund. He suggested she do the same, but he didn't push. She chose to stay the course with her own broker, assuming the broker would do the right thing and let her know if the market went sour. She had $900,000 in her IRA at the time.

Ninety-nine days later, she came home to an IRA that contained only $650,000. Her broker had let the IRA languish, and it lost $250,000, nearly a third of its original value. The wife was furious, of course, blaming the broker for failure to act and wishing she had taken her husband's advice. Fortunately, her loss was on paper only. Her original principal remained intact, but her risk tolerance is far different today and her portfolio is much safer. But she would have saved a fortune if she had used a temporary safe-retirement planning tool, such as a money-market fund, until she was available to closely monitor her risk-based assets.

The Need for Industry Reform

As I said earlier in this book, my business thrives on the development of solid relationships with my clients, as do the practices of other planners with similar philosophies. The insurance industry itself needs to build a stronger relationship with the consumer at large: you. Much consumer skepticism still exists regarding the insurance business, and rightfully so. Although I've been in the insurance business for decades, I remain skeptical about certain products myself.

This is why a few of us in the business recently began a quiet and growing movement for industry reform. We've been talking to insurance company leaders and regulators, calling for better standards for the hiring and firing of insurance representatives, sales managers, and executive personnel. We've been doing this because we see the need for a higher level of integrity and self-governing industry organizations to make it happen. You should know this, because it will help you feel justified as you maintain a watchful attitude when dealing with insurance people. It will help you feel better about demanding more consumer-friendly products, asking for detailed information about every product, and insisting on taking the time to study that information. Only then can you make your own decisions about the best and safest retirement options for you!

Registered Investment Adviser Designation

Now let's deal with another issue you should be aware of, something that's certain to cause a stir in the world of financial planning: as I mentioned earlier in the book, I think anyone dealing with OPM (that's other people's money) should be required to become a registered investment adviser (RIA). RIA licensure is granted by the U.S. Securities & Exchange Commission (SEC) after applicants pass a series of exams, and you should always ask your financial planner for documented evidence of his RIA license.

The type of knowledge RIAs are required to learn is particularly critical—not to mention required by law—for anyone who assists or counsels people on financial decisions. RIA designation also imposes an added layer of accountability on RIA licensees, because a licensee stands to lose his RIA license for various infractions. In addition, RIA training gives a professional financial planner more knowledge and investment-related flexibility, which can work in your favor.

If someone who calls herself a financial planner lacks an RIA license and tells you to move a mutual fund into an annuity, she has broken federal securities law. I don't know how many billions of dollars have been moved into annuities, but I wonder how many people have moved assets based on the advice of non-RIAs. This type of activity is rampant in the industry. The problem has grown substantially, because RIA designation requires hours of inconvenient course work for financial professionals. Many think they already know enough to give investment advice, but RIA studies would really give them an education about all types of financial vehicles, including mutual funds, stocks, bonds, real-estate insurance trusts, and all the rest.

Although the insurance industry needs to step up its efforts to require all planners to have an RIA, you need not wait for reform. My best advice to help you ensure a proper safe-retirement strategy is to ask around. Spend the time necessary to find a qualified RIA who understands safe-retirement planning.

As for industry professionals reading this book, I know this kind of advice may cause a lot of grief among our colleagues, but all of us in the industry will be better for it. If you lack an RIA license, take the time now to get properly licensed. You have no idea how much you will enjoy the additional knowledge, the professional edge, and the new confidence you'll have to improve your practice.

CHAPTER 14

Investing Safely in Your Future

CRITICS OF ANNUITIES OFTEN POINT TO THE HIGH FEES ASSO-
ciated with some products, the high commissions, and the
long surrender periods. In fact, the annuity surrender period
draws more media criticism than any other aspect of the annuity.
My argument is that not all surrender periods are alike and, yes, you
have to leave your principal in place long enough for your money
to work. Mutual funds can carry fees for early withdrawal—in fact,
some have more fees than any annuity. Yet the critics insist that you
should keep your money at risk, pay heavy fees for early withdrawal
from mutual funds, pay additional fees for so-called unbiased (hah!)
fee-based planning, and face the possibility of catastrophic losses at
the same time—all for the privilege of keeping every dime of your
gains (and losing every dime of it when the market falls). That's a
great way to lose a lot of dimes.

Fee-Based versus Commission-Based Planning

As for expensive fees, long surrender periods, and high commissions, the critics are confusing variable annuities—which tend
to have the latter—with fixed annuities. In order to confound the
public, and point consumers toward risk-bearing securities, they like
to paint every annuity with the same brush. They're simply misled by
sources in competing industries—people who are paid to warp the
truth about annuities. Unfortunately, media people hear from these
sources often, usually to single out the worst annuity on the planet
and liken it to all annuities.

As for standard annuity commissions, they are very fair. Earlier in this book, I compared annuity commissions, mutual-fund fees, and real-estate commissions. The standard commission for an annuity product I offer is around 5 to 7 percent, so it's roughly equal to a real-estate commission. Meanwhile, it galls me to hear people say that fee-based financial planning is less biased than commission-oriented planning. I simply don't accept the idea that if someone charges a flat fee for her services, her information is necessarily more accurate.

The truth is that fee- or commission-based planning, or a combination of both, does not guarantee that a planner will put your interests first. You have to feel comfortable with the character of the person you are dealing with. You must perform your own due diligence and check the reputation of that person, because in the end, it's all about the personal relationship and trust level you have with your planner. Scary, isn't it?

Fee-based planning may very well be trustworthy, but it also could be biased. If a young fee-based financial planner hasn't yet experienced the dramatic sense of loss associated with a major market crash, he may lack the empathy to look at life through the eyes of a retiree. He may give biased advice about stock-market allocations that are far more appropriate for his own age group, not yours. People in my age group—pre- and postretirees, including millions of baby boomers—need to be more concerned about not going broke before they die.

Reindel's Top 10 Mandates for Retirement Planning

There are so many things to think about, but let's focus on things that should be your most important priorities. When I first came up with this list, I was trying to separate my business into two main areas of focus. I eventually decided that my business as a safe-retirement advocate really focused on a) LTC planning and b) safe-retirement income planning. These two areas lead a list I call Reindel's Top 10 Mandates for Retirement Planning:

Protecting Assets from Nursing-Home Expenses
1. There are insurance alternatives to traditional long-term care insurance, in certain annuities and other products.

2. Annuities may be used in LTC planning.
3. Annuities may help certain clients with income needs in a long term care situation.
4. Contracts with family caregivers may help preserve assets.
5. If a home is valued over $500,000, additional planning is needed.

Avoiding Outliving Your Money
6. Avoid using stocks or mutual funds in retirement accounts.
7. A "laddered" annuity approach is a safe route to income.
8. Reverse mortgages can be a source of income for older clients.
9. Leaving assets to children should not be a major concern.
10. Failure to plan for long-term care makes income planning a pointless exercise.

As a safe-retirement advocate, I tell retirees it is essential to protect their assets from erosion through the preparation of long-term care expenses. Retirees also need to be sure their portfolios have enough guaranteed income to meet essential expenses. This can be accomplished by ensuring that your actual investment risk equals your risk tolerance at a given age, not at a particular point in a market cycle.

As I've said before, there are alternatives to traditional long-term care insurance built into some annuities and life-insurance policies. Asset gifting and the contracting of family caregivers may help preserve assets. Annuities can also be used as part of your plan in certain states. Again, check with an elder-law attorney for rules in your area. Each case is very individual and needs to be looked at carefully.

I've said all this time and again, because boomers face uncertain times. Anything goes with the balance of power. Politicians on both sides of the aisle recognize the power of the boomer vote and its persistent and steadily rising cry for health care reform. Nonetheless, many people procrastinate about income planning and long-term care until they find themselves in crisis mode, formulating a retirement strategy at the worst possible time.

When people like this come to me, they've been in denial about long-term care for a long time: "I'm hoping it doesn't happen to me, but if it does, my wife will take care of me as long as possible. Then we'll protect our assets in any legal way possible." This is the nature of crisis planning. "Come what may, whatever happens, happens." Some people are comfortable with this kind of planning, many are not, but this is the route most people are forced to take by default. Still in denial by avoiding the planning process, they really are in the crisis planning mode. Some gamble on living without a health care plan because they know not everyone will need long-term care. This notion is actually based on a statistically correct assumption—among every group of thirty or so people who attend the average financial-planning seminar, only two or three will eventually need long-term care.

The procrastination applies to general retirement planning as well: people dream about retirement for years, but most don't really begin any serious retirement planning until they're nearly ready to leave their careers. By then, they've heard about needing 70 to 100 percent of their preretirement incomes in retirement, so they ballpark a target sum and hope for the best.

That's a big mistake. The best strategy you can undertake is to know in advance what your household and lifestyle expenses are really going to be. To do this, you need to take a detailed inventory of your cost of living today and then, along with your advisor, calculate the way in which you intend to pay for some of those costs in the future. From there, you and your advisor will explore methods of paying for catastrophic illness and long-term care, if necessary. Then, you'll move on to more pleasant topics, such as your target activities in retirement: what do you want to do with your freedom?

It's a Jungle Out There

I know this sounds easy enough, but the entire planning process requires a serious effort on your part. It cannot be taken lightly, and it cannot be accomplished by conferring with friends—unless your friends are professional retirement planners. Most of us simply forget the many details a professional knows from experience that will help you through the planning maze. Unfortunately, most people wait until the last minute to plan their retirement, and this is not a good thing. Emotions run amok and panic sets in. Sometimes tempers flare and tears flow in last-minute planning sessions.

I usually face confirmation biases in my clients, where selective reasoning favors information that confirms previously held beliefs. It can be overcome, but old concepts must be challenged, especially as we enter our retirement years. Confirmation bias can lead reasonable people to reject logical advice. You simply cannot continue your previous investment and lifestyle choices and expect to achieve a healthy and safe retirement.

A good annuity contract can provide returns that come close to, or even beat, long-term returns from the market, without risk. You have to look at the entire picture to understand the value of the annuity. For example, in August 2007, ten-year returns on the Dow dropped to 4.9 percent, NASDAQ ten-year returns sank to 4.8 percent, and the S&P dipped to 4.4 percent. The year-to-date return on the S&P at that point was a paltry 1 percent. At that point in time, the types of solid annuities addressed in this book were returning to the tune of 5 percent to 7 percent—all without a cent of risk to principal!

Am I getting through? By August 2007, the average American's 401(k) account was still heavily leveraged in stocks—usually about two-thirds of each portfolio. Changes were afoot, however—a third of each portfolio, on average, had been moved to **stable-value assets**, such as annuities, money-market accounts, and bonds. Even among newly hired workers, the change was evident: stable-value assets represented 24 percent of assets in the portfolios of these workers, up from 19 percent in 2005. In 1998, newly hired workers on average had only 7 percent of their portfolios in stable-value assets.

Yet many people still refuse to believe that the stock market is basically a rigged game. Of course, not everyone in the market is colluding to steal your money. In fact, many of the experts you see on television are some of the best financial minds in the nation, people who truly believe in tackling issues ethically. They are highly trained, superbly educated people with some of the best institutions in the country. When I say the stock market is a rigged system, I mean the average person cannot win in the long run without the help of a true expert.

To win in the stock market, you must follow the technical and analytical aspects of trading on an almost hourly basis. You have to be nimble, constantly watchful, and very, very careful. You cannot survive in the stock market through blind investment. You must find a great broker—and there are some out there. But there are also countless silver-tongued charlatans on the equities playing field.

We all know what the charlatans will tell you—the route to riches in the market is to buy low and sell high. They will tell you how easy it is for them to do this on your behalf. But here's the reality of buyers and sellers on each side of any transaction. The smart buyer is able to acquire the best talent in the business, and the poor schmuck on the other side of the transaction gets the shaft. The "little guy" in this story will eventually sell low in a market downdraft. The smart buyer then becomes a smart seller, when the best talent in the business tells her when to sell. See? It's a rigged game.

The best players in the stock market are a lofty breed. They follow a different rule book. They hope you will believe what you read in the media, because they generally have other plans for their wealthy clientele. Media reports are sometimes fueled (and their report-ers fooled) by disinformation deliberately leaked, fed, and sourced through blogs and other less-than-trustworthy conduits in order to obscure the truth.

I say, "*Caveat emptor.* Buyers and readers beware." Don't blame the reporters. It's up to you to evaluate your own investment options through reliable professional sources. There are all sorts of people out there ready and willing to take your money: planners, stockbrokers, attorneys, CPAs—you name it. In this book, I've cited many exam-ples of professionals caught in the act of professional misconduct and outright fraud. I've seen the costly process of creating family trusts when no trust was needed. Some attorneys aggressively push trusts at seminars, even trying to sell trusts to people with only $50,000 in assets. Those people don't need trusts! That's overkill. They fork over $2,500 or more for trust paperwork, and in the end, their children wind up paying an attorney to get them out of the trust.

Most people attend financial seminars hoping to find someone they can trust. Attendees may initially sign up for the free lunch, but I know they also come to my seminars to check me out. Even without much experience, a person could probably stand up there, talk financial-ese in a kind and patient tone of voice, and still get some people to come in for a consultation. The challenge I face is to separate myself and my considerable professional experience from the pack. Other truly qualified professionals, such as stockbrokers, attorneys and financial planners, face the same dilemma. A seminar is often the best way to let people know who we are. Unfortunately, there are plenty of less experienced people in this business who know how to dazzle seminar attendees. Like I said before, caveat emptor.

Reindel's Five Basic Qualifications of a Good Financial Advisor

That said, I offer you Reindel's Five Basic Qualifications of a Good Financial Advisor.

1. *Trustworthiness*. How will you know whether someone is trustworthy or not? Ask his former clients. Find out if you can contact several current or former clients. You can also contact the National Ethics Bureau or your local Better Business Bureau, and you can also check with your state insurance department and division of securities. If you still can't obtain the information you need, look out!

2. *Knowledge and expertise*. Any advisor you consider should be an SEC-licensed RIA. It also may be acceptable for a person to be an investment advisor representative registered with an RIA firm, depending on the firm and the level of supervision the advisor representative receives from other in-house RIAs. The firm's RIA designation will be clearly stated on the advisor representative's business card.

3. *The wherewithal to always keep the client's best interest at the forefront*. Do the planner's recommendations really provide for safe-retirement income, guaranteed principal, and other elements discussed in this book? She may suggest certain risk-related investments, if legally licensed to do so, but is the overall strategy aimed at preserving your peace of mind without venturing into inappropriately excessive long-term risk?

4. *Years of experience*. If you can't seem to get a straight answer on this one, be polite but find the office door as soon as possible.

Experience counts. Every safe-retirement advocate I train has solid career experience and a verifiable background.

5. *A commitment to service clients.* Ask a lot of questions about this one. How many meetings per year can you expect? What about telephone access? Are there other truly qualified professionals in the office who are able to help if your consultant happens to be out of town? How many people will be available to process payouts or intercede with providers if necessary? How often can you expect to see written financial summaries specifically related to *your* portfolio? Will you be able to meet with your advisor as often as necessary to always have peace of mind? These are questions you should be asking yourself or your advisor. But you can't always be sure until you're there, dealing with the advisor on a daily basis.

In this business, reputation is everything, so I always question my own business practices. Am I doing the right thing? Can I do better? Do I have the latest information regarding the best new innovations in the annuity industry? Self-evaluation is a constant process for a good financial planner.

From time to time, clients leave financial decisions entirely up to me. For example, a recent retiree turned her entire $1.2 million 401(k) over to me and told me to create a retirement plan for her. I also conferred with other qualified professionals, including her accountant. Over time, in fact, I had numerous meetings with her accountant, who validated every move I made. Yet more than a few in this business would simply take the money and make a steady stream of cavalier moves into a mixed bag of assets, reaping hefty commissions along the way.

My fundamental goal with her 401(k) was to provide her with guaranteed income for life, preserve her principal, and diversify her investments into other safe investment vehicles. Like other reputable planners, I take safety very seriously, and my clients know it. Some potential clients have come to me with risky investments in mind and I have gently shown them the door. To remain a bona fide safe-retirement advocate, I've occasionally been obligated to turn down business. I am that serious about asset safety for retirement portfolios, and anyone you use for investment advice should be, too.

Fraud

The telltale signs of fraud become apparent over time, beginning with questions left unanswered—or worse yet, breezy and evasive statements followed by an expression designed to deter you from asking another question. Once, a friend of mine set up an IRA with a nationally recognized brokerage, one of the biggest names in the business. His broker seemed very knowledgeable and professional, and things were fine—for a while. Then my friend learned that the broker had left the company. Without anyone asking for his permission, his accounts had been transferred to another broker. But the real shocker came in a newspaper headline: his original broker had defrauded an investor, and that's why he was no longer with the company.

In another case, the owner of an investment firm in Connecticut recently admitted to using $4 million of his clients' assets to gamble, take lavish vacations, and buy expensive cars. In U.S. District Court, he pled guilty to ten counts of mail fraud, one count of embezzlement from an employee benefit plan, and four counts of filing false tax returns. This very same individual had provided insurance and financial services to a stable of more than 200 clients for many years.

The investment firm owner had told his clients he would guarantee an 8 percent return for money invested in a fixed investment account under his control. His clients entrusted him with a combined $5.5 million as a result. Unfortunately, that fixed investment account was fictitious and blatant fraud. Instead of investing the money, the planner put the money into his own business and personal bank accounts. To cover his tracks, he mailed fictitious monthly financial statements to his investors.

Look out for the following warning signs of fraud.

Phony documentation. In the case involving the phony fixed investment account, the planner crafted phony statements bearing his own letterhead, rather than those of an account provider. You must pay careful attention to the documentation you receive from planners and brokers.

Contracts. Any of your questions regarding contracts demand succinct, readily available, and easily understood answers. The length of annuity contracts varies dramatically, with some exceeding 120 pages. If a contract's terminology is anything less than crystal clear, you should immediately seek a second opinion about the product, perhaps from your attorney or accountant. Naturally, most contracts seem long and tediously detailed, but I'll try to get you started with some pointers.

Only a contract for a fixed annuity, for example, would mention a guaranteed rate of return. Variable annuities and fixed-indexed annuities obviously offer ever-changing possibilities of returns. Further, you may find precious little speculation in variable or fixed-indexed contracts as to how the annuities would perform in the long run. You might find only a stated minimum guarantee of return, which should be found on the declarations page (often referred to as the "dec page") of the annuity contract.

Any form of fixed annuity contract should readily provide such information, along with the variety of crediting options mentioned earlier, if you are considering fixed-indexed annuities. If not, ask for direction from the presenter, but settle for nothing less than proof in written form, and be sure the contract's minimum crediting options clearly explain how future earnings and credits would be allocated in your annuity account. Again, this information should be found on the declarations page of your annuity contract. (As for probable rates of return for variable annuities, you are on your own.)

Surrender charges should also be found on the declarations page, along with a listing of the annuity's various liquidity features (as mentioned in other chapters). Here you will also find additional information about the annuity provider, the contract inception date, the name and description of the annuity product itself, amounts of premium deposits, any future premiums that are due, and other related data, all of which should be found within the first three pages of the contract. If extra fees are attached, they would cover additionally purchased contract riders. But unlike a real-estate sales/purchase contract, don't bother looking for listed agent commissions, which are paid by the insurance carrier.

Inaccessibility. Another red flag is accessibility. How easy or difficult is it to get in touch with your financial advisors? How informative or helpful are they? When you ask specific questions, are the answers evasive? Do they defer your questions, trying to placate you with remarks like, "I'll find out and get back to you," for days or weeks on end? If you cannot reach your planner because she never returns your calls, or if your broker gives conflicting or confusing answers to your questions, beware. You have the right to ask hard questions and receive prompt, detailed answers. When it comes to contract review, you have every right to consult an attorney—particularly someone who specializes in financial contract law.

All of these situations could be signs of managerial incompetence, leading to costly errors. They could also be signs of legal, but unethical, actions by the broker. Such evasiveness could indicate that inappropriate actions have been taken on behalf of the client. For example, if a planner has placed his client's money in investment vehicles that are inappropriate, such vehicles may be hard to detect without a second professional opinion. Trust your instincts, and get that second opinion. You are always entitled to seek additional information about your investments from a variety of sources. If you develop even a vaguely uneasy feeling about the person with whom you have entrusted your money, do something about it and confer with another professional.

How else can you tell the difference between a poor advisor and one who is trustworthy? Generally, untrustworthy advisors will try to recommend inappropriate annuities with high surrender charges and no liquidity. Certainly, no unethical advisor would send a client to one of my seminars—or to the seminar of any other ethical advocate—but the clients come anyway, because they suspect a problem. They wisely seek a fresh perspective.

When does the seed of suspicion begin to grow? Another classic sign of inappropriate advice is when an advisor claims to have an easy, one-stop solution for your every financial need. This is classic advice from a rip-off artist. There is no single miracle product that would handle a retiree's every need, be it a mutual fund, an annuity, a stock, or a life-insurance policy.

CHAPTER 15

A Look into the Future

A FUNDAMENTAL PART OF THE ADVISOR'S JOB, IN MY OPINION, is to look at the client's financial holdings and see if his recommendations fit that particular client's situation, risk tolerance, and goals. If clients come to me with a yen for high risk and claim to have had a positive experience with that approach, I won't try to change their minds. Instead, I'll invite them to come back and see me if their risk tolerance changes in the future.

So I don't have all the answers for everyone. I am a specialist in annuities. Beware the advisor who seems to have all the answers, or the advisor who believes that the secret to wealth is investing all of one's eggs in one basket, whether it may hold securities, bonds, or any other financial instrument. And those of us with ethical business practices will tell you straightaway that we specialize in particular areas pertaining to specific instruments, investments, insurance products, and so on.

When you hear securities analysts tout stock investments on business news shows, you might think they're encouraging viewers to have total immersion in the market. Actually, that's not what they're saying at all. People on TV are enthusiastically talking about the areas in which they have expertise. Like me, they're excited about the knowledge they have. They love what they do. But you must take what they say with a grain of salt, and understand where they are coming from.

What's Next

In this economic climate, we all must remain vigilant. I think the stock market will be schizophrenic for the next fifteen years. Historically, the average bull market has lasted around ten to twenty years, and the average secular bear market has historically remained intact for the same time period. The last great bull market lasted from 1982 to 2000. There have been major downturns during bull markets and major rallies during bear markets (with many analysts calling 2005 to 2008 a good rally period, or short-term bull market, in a bear market). During the last bear market, which ran from 1966 to 1982, stocks lost about 10 percent of their value. If we are, in fact, in a bear market, it may take ten to fifteen years for the market to recover to the levels of the last bull market.

Such a stock market trend will cause people using market-based investments to run out of money, especially if those instruments are used for income planning. Many retired investors may have to return to work or move in with their children. During these hard times, annuities will become increasingly important to investors and will once again become the respected mainstream planning tools they have been in the past.

Unfortunately, this will not happen until an intra-industry battle runs its course. A battle continues to rage between the insurance industry and the equities industry, and it will worsen before it improves. I believe the outcome will ultimately favor the underdog annuity, because the next bull market is a long way off. The consumer's ever-increasing savvy will recognize the current criticism of the annuity for what it is: nothing more than a smokescreen. People will eventually recognize annuities for what they truly are: the safest, most secure investments you can make for your overall retirement income plan.

As for IRAs and 401(k)s, they generally make for solid retirement planning tools and should be used to accumulate retirement income safely. They were designed for this purpose, and as a safe-retirement advocate, I would recommend them to anyone. But when it comes time to retire, more than a few people should remove their retirement accounts from the market. Their assets should be secured in a safe, tax-deferred place as always, and used for income as needed.

That's my opinion. I leave the rest for you to consider. But I also strongly suggest that you take your hand off the pause button long before your retirement. Secure an appropriate portion of your assets against catastrophic loss, and I know you will live well and prosper in what should rightfully be the very best years of your life.

GLOSSARY

Accumulation cycle: The period of time during which annuities accumulate compounded, tax-deferred earnings, which eventually lead to income payments for the annuity policyholder.

Accumulation unit: Often related to variable annuities, these represent a proportionate share of the net assets of an insurance carrier's given investment portfolio. Say an insurance company's portfolio is worth $20 million. If the company decides to split up its $20 million into four million separate accumulation units, each unit would be worth $5. As investment advisors hired by the insurance company increase the worth of the company's portfolio, each accumulation unit increases in value accordingly. For example, if the portfolio grows from $20 million to $25 million, the accumulation units would grow from being worth $5 to being worth $6.25 each.

Accumulation value: The accumulation value of an annuity is the combined amount of interest earned and added to the original principal contribution by the annuity owner.

Administrative charges: These are fees for items such as data management and other expenses, and they may be charged as flat fees—with or without early withdrawals. This charge is often listed in a variable annuity contract as being based on a percentage (around 0.15 percent annually) of your total account value. In such a case, your administrative fees grow with the value of your variable annuity account, with a $20,000 account generating $30 in annual fees.

Annuitization/annuitizing: A term commonly related to more traditional annuities, annuitization refers to the act of beginning income payments to the annuity holder and the end of the accumulation phase of the traditional annuity.

Annuitization distribution: This term is another way to describe the action of beginning the distribution, or payout/payment, of income from an annuity contract. This phase generally begins after contract maturity. However, existing and emerging forms of modern annuities offer more payout flexibility.

Annuitization methods: Annuitization basically means the moment when accumulation ends and distribution begins. Annuitization methods are payout options, payout/income schedules, and other features, which can be found at any point within a contract or specifically within the "Annuitization Options at Maturity" section of a contract.

Annuitization options at maturity (section of contract): This part of the annuity contract spells out payouts, payout options, and walk-away bonus/cash-out options at the end of the contract term.

Beneficiary restriction form: Upon the death of an annuity holder, any payouts to the beneficiary can be fully or partially restricted by completing this form. This can dictate payments for a certain period of time rather than specific distribution of a lump sum, which may be desirable for certain types of beneficiaries.

Bonus product: An annuity that offers a cash-bonus addition to the annuity account, usually upon the purchase and signing of the annuity contract, although the bonus may not be fully available until the annuity matures.

Cap: A maximum limit placed on earnings in an annuity contract, which allows policyholders to share in a percentage of market gains up to a designated point. The cap is determined by what it costs the company to buy the option.

Confirmation bias: A phenomenon wherein people focus on information that confirms previously held beliefs and ignore information that contradicts those beliefs.

Consumer-leveraged products: Another term for consumer-friendly, or consumer-favorable, products.

Distribution: A routine schedule of payments made to policyholders in the income, or distribution, phase of the annuity contract.

Earnings: The monies earned from investments made by the insurance company on behalf of the annuity policyholder, which are then added to the policyholder's annuity account.

Earnings caps: Earnings limitations placed on annuity accounts participating in index activity, in exchange for risk-free guarantees of principal, earnings, lifetime income, and so on.

Emerging payout options: Annuities are offering more flexibility regarding payout methods, including the option of receiving income for life while allowing the balance of principal to grow through earnings in the form of "index" credits—earnings based on a market "index"—without risking principal or prior earnings. This is available through the guaranteed lifetime-income optional rider. Some carriers charge a fee for this type of feature.

Equity-indexed annuity: When initially offered as an innovative product, the fixed-indexed annuity was sometime erroneously called an equity-indexed annuity, giving consumers the impression that the fixed-indexed annuity was some kind of equity product—which it is not. The fixed-indexed annuity guarantees principal and a set rate of annual earnings, along with additional earnings (or not) based on index performance.

Excessive commission: An arbitrary figure based on assessments of high and low commissions received by annuity salespeople for annuity sales.

Fixed annuities: Annuities that offer a fixed interest rate that compounds each year to grow the amount of principal in the account. This principal is guaranteed and can never be lost.

Fixed-indexed annuities: Insurance products that offer consumers the option of choosing how they would like to have earnings credited to their accounts. All or part of earnings credited to an annuity account may be set at a fixed rate of interest every year, or earnings may be based upon the performance of a chosen market index. Most carriers allow annuity owners to reallocate the way their earnings are credited once a year.

Fixed-period method: The annuity holder receives equal monthly income payments during a fixed time period, usually five to thirty years. Payments continue until the end of the fixed period and then stop forever. If the annuity holder dies during this fixed period, his beneficiary could continue to receive payments until the payment period is completed in full.

Guaranteed (growth) income account value: The amount of money accumulated, compounded, and added to principal in an annuity account for the purpose of generating an income stream. When the annuity owner is ready to begin receiving income, the total accumulated value of the account determines the amount of money to be paid out as income for the life of the contract owner. The higher it is, the more you get.

Guaranteed lifetime-income withdrawal benefit: A benefit that is achieved through the purchase of an additional contract rider that states that an account used solely for income will be guaranteed to grow at a certain percentage, rate compounding, until the consumer decides to begin receiving income from the annuity. Once the annuity owner begins receiving income, the owner is guaranteed a fixed income for life, an amount that will never decrease. While the income is deducted from the annuity account each year, the balance of the account may continue to earn interest, allowing continued growth while also providing a fixed income.

Guaranteed minimum income benefit: A benefit that can be purchased and made part of an annuity contract to provide a guaranteed minimum payment of steady income to the annuity policyholder after a given period of time.

Immediate annuities: These are also called single-premium income annuities, or SPIAs. They can provide a lifetime of income for an annuity policyholder, income for a specific amount of time, or a number of variations; payouts for any or all combinations begin from a month to a year after the policyholder contributes a one-time deposit.

Immediate premium bonus: A type of bonus usually added to the annuity buyer's principal the first day the buyer signs the annuity contract. Be sure to read the fine print, however, because the bonus could come with various stipulations, high surrender charges, and so on.

Income: In the annuity industry, income is the routine payment, or distribution, of money that goes to the annuity policyholder after certain types of annuities mature; in the case of the immediate annuity, income may be received almost immediately after signing the annuity contract.

Index credits: Earnings added to an annuity account that are a part of the earnings made by the insurance carrier based on the performance of a market index. Some annuities feature optional riders that allow index earnings to continue while the owner receives income.

Insurance-industry rating services: The stability of insurance companies and their products are monitored by independent rating companies, which give insurance companies performance ratings based on product safety and other factors. Two of these services are A.M. Best and Morningstar; they are easily found on the Internet. Companies with good ratings (such as A+ or A) are proud to display their rankings.

Life-annuity method: With this method, the life-annuity holder receives a steady, dependable sum of money each month for her entire lifetime. Upon her death, all payments stop and the annuity carrier is not obligated to make further payments to heirs.

Lifetime-income rider: See *Guaranteed lifetime-income withdrawal benefit.*

Long-term asset-allocation strategy: Also known as the diversified-portfolio strategy, this essentially is the long-established buy-and-hold concept of participation in risk-based equity markets. This strategy was finally proven vulnerable—and fatally so for many investors—during the economic crisis that began in 2008. Long-term annuity strategies may sound similar to asset-allocation strategies, but most annuity strategies avoid risk of principal, earnings, and lifetime income. The two must never be confused.

Long-term care (LTC) insurance: Provides various levels of coverage to pay for nursing-home care, with premiums most affordable at a young age. Some annuity riders and life-insurance policies also provide alternative methods of funding nursing-home care.

Market value adjustment (MVA): A feature that allows an annuity owner to share the risk of his potential early surrender prior to the contract's date of maturity. While formulas vary, the MVA triggers an increase in surrender charges as overall market interest rates fall during various economic conditions. As interest rates rise, surrender fees fall according to MVA terms in the contract. MVAs only apply when surrender penalties would apply as defined in a section of the contract commonly referred to as MVAs.

Mixed allocation: This means that monies in an annuity account can be applied to—or allocated to—a variety of earning methods, including accumulation through a fixed rate of interest *and* accumulation through index participation.

Mortality/expense-risk fee: Found with some variable annuities, this fee typically runs about 1 percent to 1.25 percent of the policyholder's account value and covers various risks and costs assumed by the insurance carrier, including sales commissions and risk exposure.

Multiyear guaranteed annuity (MYGA): This annuity resembles a bank CD in that it offers a set rate of return guaranteed for a specific period of time.

No-fee withdrawal allowance: In contracts and marketing materials, this allowance is termed a penalty-free withdrawal. It is an amount of money that may be withdrawn each year from an annuity account without incurring surrender penalties. For example, if the annuity owner's principal contribution is $100,000, no interest has yet been added to the owner's principal, and the withdrawal allowance is 10 percent per year, the annuity owner would be allowed to withdraw $10,000 during that year.

Nonbonus products: Products that do not come with a premium, or signing, bonus. They may initially sound unattractive, but such products may offer considerably higher upside potential.

Nursing-home rider: A rider that allows the withdrawal of certain amounts of money—or access up to 100 percent of an annuity balance—penalty free for nursing-home expenses.

Participation rate: As an option for crediting earnings gains to her account, the participation rate allows the annuity owner to share in a stated percentage of the upward movement of an index. For example, if the index is up 10 percent and the annuity contract has a participation rate of 70 percent, the contract would receive a credit of 7 percent.

Payout schedule: Industry jargon for the method in which income from an annuity may be distributed to the policyholder. Upon maturity, income payments, or payouts, can be routinely received for life or for a set period of years. While many people choose to receive monthly income payouts/payments, payouts can be received quarterly, annually, or semiannually, depending on carrier policies and consumer needs.

Point-to-point (crediting) method: A method of calculating annual annuity-account earnings starting at the beginning point of a given year and concluding at the end point of the same year.

Premium: A payment, or a regularly scheduled series of payments, made to an insurance company in exchange for the benefits of owning an insurance policy.

Premium bonus: A monetary bonus provided by an insurance carrier to the annuity buyer as an incentive to purchase an annuity. The premium bonus is usually a percentage of the amount of principal contribution—or the initial premium contribution—made by the buyer. If a buyer contributes $100,000, and the carrier adds a 10 percent premium bonus, the value of the buyer's annuity account would increase to $110,000 either immediately or at some point during or after the duration of the annuity contract.

Principal: In the annuity industry, principal typically is the lump-sum initial contribution added to an annuity account by the annuity policyholder. In fixed and fixed-indexed annuities, in particular, principal is guaranteed from loss or reduction due to market activity. All earnings are added to principal to compound or accelerate the rate of future earnings of the account.

Rate of interest earnings: The percentage rate of interest to be earned by an annuity account, which can be fixed and guaranteed with certain types of annuities.

Registered investment adviser (RIA): After completing studies and exams required for proper licensing, an RIA registers with his state securities department and/or the SEC by filing Form ADV. RIAs typically register with the SEC when they manage more than $25 million in assets.

Reset: When a contract reaches its annual anniversary date and any gains are credited and locked in, a new starting point begins for credits in the following 365-day period, or "year." These events are called annual resets, which lock in gains every year. Other options allow resets every two or more years.

Return-of-premium feature: This feature allows for the total refund of premiums, or principal, if the annuity owner is unhappy with the annuity for any reason. Such features may require that a premium bonus and/or interest earnings be forfeited in order for the premium to be returned.

Riders: These extra benefit provisions are described in additional documents that are attached to the main annuity contract. Such extra benefits, if not included as a feature of the main annuity contract, can be purchased for additional fees.

Safe-Retirement Incomer: An intermingling of income annuities, fixed annuities, and fixed-indexed annuities in a retirement portfolio, which provide immediate income, guaranteed safety of principal, a fixed rate of earnings, and a limited, or capped, rate of participation in the market.

Sales loads: Trading fees commonplace in the industry that are charged when parts of a client's account are transferred to and from various investments.

Signing bonus: A synonym for premium bonus, because such bonuses are usually offered by insurance carriers to annuity buyers upon signing the annuity contract. It can be added to the annuity buyer's initial principal contribution either immediately, during the course of the maturity period, or upon maturity.

Single premium: Used to fund most fixed and fixed-indexed annuities, this is a single, lump-sum contribution, or premium, put into an annuity account.

Single-premium income annuities (SPIAs): Also called immediate annuities, SPIAs require a one-time deposit and deliver guaranteed income for life or for a specified period of time determined by the annuity owner. Income payouts can begin almost immediately but must commence within the first year.

Spread: A crediting method in which the annuity owner chooses to forfeit a percentage of index performance. For example, if the crediting option has a 1 percent spread and the index is up 8 percent, then the account is credited 7 percent. This modification helps the insurance provider assume risk and guarantee principal and earnings for annuity owners.

Springing power of attorney: A form of power of attorney that only comes into play if the person in question becomes incapacitated.

Stable-value assets: Assets with a stable, or dependable, value, such as money-market funds, bank CDs, certain types of annuities, and other products.

Stepped-up death benefit: An increase in the death benefit for beneficiaries following various formulas.

Surrender charges: Fees paid to the insurance company for early withdrawal of monies from an annuity account that exceeds the allowable level of annual withdrawals. Most annuities allow penalty-free withdrawals of up to 10 percent per year of the total value of the account. Any monies withdrawn in addition to the 10 percent penalty-free withdrawal would incur a surrender charge.

Surrender value: The amount of money in an annuity account that the annuity owner could walk away with after surrender charges have been subtracted.

Term (life) insurance: Probably the least costly and most simplistic form of life insurance, term-life policies require a regular installment-type payment called a premium, which is often paid by the policyholder on a monthly or yearly basis. In effect for a specific term, or period of time, coverage under the term-life policy might also be terminated when the policyholder reaches a certain age. The term insurance policy pays the coverage amount stated in the policy, usually to a beneficiary, if the policyholder dies during the coverage term, or period. If the policyholder lives beyond the term stated in the policy, this type of insurance policy pays nothing. Unlike other forms of insurance, including whole-life insurance, premium costs are low at first and may increase with the age of the policyholder.

Terminal-illness rider: Most annuities allow substantial withdrawals of money or access to the entire value of the account, penalty free, from an annuity account given a terminal-illness diagnosis.

Traditional annuities: Purchased for a defined period of time, these annuities divulge the annuity's rate of interest to be added to principal for *only* the first year. All subsequent interest rates were essentially unknown for the remainder of the contract period. Annuities have since been modernized, adding far greater transparency, flexibility, and consumer-friendly features.

Underlying fund expenses: Fees paid by the policyholder through the insurance company to the mutual-fund managers who handle the investments purchased on your behalf by the insurance company. In the securities industry, these include trading fees for transferring part of an account from one investment option to another.

Unemployment rider: This emerging annuity feature allows the penalty-free withdrawal of money from the annuity account if the owner becomes unemployed.

Universal life insurance: This type of life-insurance policy combines the benefits of an adjustable premium, acts like a savings account, and can be flexible. For example, a death benefit can increase or decrease or last for longer or shorter periods of time, depending on the amount of premium you put into the policy. The contract builds cash value over time as you pay premiums, and cash can be withdrawn.

Variable annuities: An annuity with an array of investment combinations that resemble the asset-allocation strategies seen in mutual funds and other investment packages. Some may offer investments in stocks and/or bonds. Any combination of investment may vary widely in terms of risk, overall quality of performance, profit/loss ratios, and other factors common among instruments in the securities market.

Walk-away premium bonus: A type of bonus often immediately added to the annuity buyer's account and available to the buyer at any time, even if the buyer opts to terminate the annuity during or after the first year of the annuity contract. The annuity owner would therefore "walk away" with the bonus but may still incur surrender charges. The walk-away bonus helps alleviate the impact of surrender charges.